SINGLE
Mamahood

SINGLE
Mamahood

✳ ✳ ✳ ✳ ✳

Advice and Wisdom
for the African-American
Single Mother

KELLY WILLIAMS

A CITADEL PRESS BOOK
Published by Carol Publishing Group

To Winston

Copyright © 1998 Kelly Williams

A Citadel Press Book
Published by Carol Publishing Group
Citadel Press is a registered trademark of Carol Communications, Inc.

Editorial, sales and distribution, rights and permissions inquiries should be addressed to Carol Publishing Group, 120 Enterprise Avenue, Secaucus, N.J. 07094.

In Canada: Canadian Manda Group, One Atlantic Avenue, Suite 105, Toronto, Ontario M6K 3E7

Carol Publishing Group books may be purchased in bulk at special discounts for sales promotion, fund-raising, or educational purposes. Special editions can be created to specifications. For details, contact Special Sales Department, Carol Publishing Group, 120 Enterprise Avenue, Secaucus, N.J. 07094.

Manufactured in the United States of America

10 9 8 7 6 5 4 3 2

Library of Congress Cataloging-in-Publication Data

Williams, Kelly
    Single mamahood : advice and wisdom for the African-American
single mother / Kelly Williams.
        p. cm.
    "A Citadel Press book."
    ISBN 0–8065–1978–9 (pb)
    1. Afro-American single mothers.   2. Single-parent family—United
States.   I. Title.
HQ759.915.W56   1998
306.85'6—dc21   97–45540
                                                           CIP

Contents

Acknowledgments

My heartfelt thanks to: Rhonda and Peter, Kim, Kyle, Ray, Kerry, Jimmy, Billy, Mom and Leon, Sonya, Stella, and Daddy

My biggest thanks goes to Winston, my inspiration, the center of my world, without whom none of this would be possible.

Introduction

I'm sitting in my Toyota Celica convertible watching my ten-year-old son, Winston, play baseball. The sun's gone down, and it's about eighty degrees. Nights like these are why so many major-league teams choose Florida for spring training.

This is a new field. There are three baseball diamonds. It's northeast St. Petersburg, home of old St. Petersburg money. It's also where Winston and I live.

I jokingly refer to my house as located in the "low-rent" district of Placido Bayou, an exclusive gated community. I live in a patio home, another term for a one-story townhouse. I bought it four years ago for $103,000. But houses in Placido Bayou run into the half-million-dollar range. My son plays baseball with kids of white moms and dads who own those homes. They also show up at baseball games to cheer their kids on. Often the dads are living out their own fantasies of playing in the major leagues. They can be hard on their sons. But at least they're there.

This is the first time I've ever felt sorry for my son for not having his father there.

He just missed a pop fly in left field, and he's beating himself up. After a couple of kids from the other team come in, there's finally a third out, and Winston's team heads for the dugout.

Winston sits all alone. He's the only black kid on the team. And he's the only one whose dad or stepdad or mom's boyfriend isn't there. Or at least that's how it seems to him—and to me, for that matter.

Drew's dad, Harvey, is one of the coaches. Harvey's sitting next to his son on the bench giving him a pep talk. Winston turns his head toward them but pretends not to really care. I know my son so well, I know what he's thinking—what he's feeling. He wishes his dad were there.

I'm choking back tears. I've honestly never felt this pain. I've been a single mama for nine years, but this feeling is a new one. Single mamas have to be ready for the unexpected.

If you want to be successful at single mamahood, you'd better first accept the fact that you are, in fact, a single mother. In other words, do not go about your life as if you're single "just for now," or "just until I find Mr. Right." Nor should you think of yourself as simply single with no children. If you do not live your single-mamahood life as if you're in it for the long haul, your children will suffer.

The sooner you accept your status as a single mama, the sooner your children will accept it. And the sooner your child will be able to develop a strong sense of self, based on what is, not on what could have been or what will be in the future. Same goes for you, Mama.

It is difficult to accept that you, alone, have the responsibility of bringing up children in this crazy world. Every African-American mother knows the challenges. With our sons, we worry about school, gangs, and girls. With our girls, it's school, boys, and men. We know the challenges we faced; we know the challenges our brothers faced. We realize little has changed from generation to generation. We understand what our children are up against. As a single African-American woman, you know the challenges are compounded with stereotypes you must rise above about kids of single mamas. You know everyone will expect your child to be a failure in school, a criminal, and a teen parent at some point.

This Father's Day, when I called home to wish Leon (my stepfather) a happy Father's Day, my sister, Kim, got on the phone to wish me a happy Father's Day. I thought it was cute. But later, after giving it some thought, I said to myself, "I'm not a father. I can never be a father to my child. All I can be is a super single mama."

That's what this book is about. It's about how women who are raising their children without the kids' father in the home can be the best parents they can possibly be. It's about how to be a super single mama.

Children raised by single mamas disproportionately represent those who engage in criminal activity, who score on the lower end of standardized achievement tests, and who are most likely to become single parents as teens. If you study the family trees of many single mamas, you'll find that single mamahood can be an endless cycle. This book attempts to offer ways to break the cycle.

Single Mamahood does not condone the institution of single mothering, but acknowledges and deals with it in an honest, realistic manner. It offers, through lessons from single mamas who are living the life every day, ways to make single mamahood work for the mothers and the children.

I'm not a doctor or a counselor. I am a journalist and a single mother. At the start of this book, my son, Winston, was approaching his seventh birthday. I completed it just shy of his eleventh, and I still don't pretend to know everything there is to know about being a parent, let alone a single mother.

I will, however, share with you some of my experiences and the stories of other single mothers to help you learn from our mistakes. My mother always told me it's easier to learn from others' mistakes than it is to make all the mistakes yourself. I believe that.

I became a single mother in 1986, when my son, Winston, came into my life. A year and a half later, his father, Teddy, and I married. During most of my single mamahood, I had not fully come to terms with my status. In fact, my shame in being "another statistic" was the motivating drive for my getting married.

Although I loved my son's father, I did not like him. I did not feel loved and I was not loving in return. (The details of the relationship are another story, one, as I have assured Teddy, that will stay in the past.) Seven months after we ran to the courthouse in downtown Los Angeles to sanctify our union, we separated. Shortly thereafter I filed for divorce.

Once again, I was a single mother. Only this time, I was proud of who and what I was. To me, that's the key. Despite how you become a single mother, be proud. As a single woman bringing up a child in this world, you must have a strong sense of yourself—high self-esteem. With it, you and your children will have the extra edge single mothers and their children need to face life's challenges.

Whether America likes it or not, single mamas are a fact of life. True, many single mamas are poor and unemployed. But growing numbers of them are working and middle class. Our country depends upon the success of these women who are single-handedly supporting their families and rearing their children.

Single mamas rely on informal advice from one another when they face difficulties parenting their children. Now and then, we'll run across a magazine article about single parenting. But much of the published material speaks to working mothers or parenting in general. Little of it is targeted to single mamas.

Perhaps the population explosion of America's single mamas has gone practically unaddressed by parenting experts because single mamahood is still one of our country's dirty little secrets. It is as if all the experts quietly hope all of us will one day find a man and solve our problem.

Fact is, that attitude contributes to many of the problems single mamas must deal with every day. Single mamas often feel so guilty, ashamed, and desperate, that instead of focusing on our children, we're out looking for a man. Society must stop putting this kind of pressure on single mamas; it only compounds the problem and sidesteps real-life issues.

This book does not attempt to glamorize or glorify single mamas—it just tells it like it is. It brings the institution out of the closet so that together, we can learn how to give our children every advantage they deserve.

As a young girl, I never in my wildest dreams expected to be a single mama. The first girl I knew who got pregnant was a beautiful ninth-grader named Hazra. One day, while I was hanging out with a couple of my tenth-grade classmates, Hazra walked by the school, wheeling her baby. She was so beautiful but so young, I felt sorry for her, thought about all the dreams she must have had that were shattered by her pregnancy. I thought she'd probably never make it through high school, let alone college. Certainly, I believed at the time, a man who wanted to be successful wouldn't have anything to do with her.

I realize now how my limited experiences put me in a position of playing judge and placing limits on Hazra's life. I know now that single mamas can do anything they want. They can finish high school and college. They can become successful in their professional lives. They can date nice men. They can be good mothers. But I was right about one thing—being a single mama is not easy.

Women become single mamas several ways. They may be unmarried when their children are born, they can get divorced after their children are born, they can adopt children while they're single, or they may be widowed before or after their children are born. Despite how you became a single mama, *Single Mamahood* can help you reduce your risk of parenting errors. The hope is you'll learn from the mistakes and successes of some of the single mamas who've shared their stories with me for this book.

SINGLE
Mamahood

A Single Mama Is...

single, separated, divorced, or widowed.

able to set and achieve goals.

perfectly capable of functioning without a husband or boyfriend.

an excellent mother.

1

Dealing With Daddy

Once I heard an interview on *Good Morning America* with Grant Hill of the Detroit Pistons and his father, Calvin Hill, former NFL runningback. They were talking about the special bond between a father and a child. Calvin said "Nothing works like a father" to give a child the "social armor he needs to make it in the world." The two Hills agreed that a father should be involved with his children, that their bond allows children to feel fully protected. I agree with them. I believe children who have both parents in the home have a leg up on children of single mamas. The next best thing to a two-parent home is giving your child as much contact with his or her father as you possibly can.

Fortunately, many single mamas involve their children's fathers in the kids' lives. But not always. That's a problem.

We have to understand that our children have the right to love their fathers, despite how we feel about them. To take this right away from our children robs them of an opportunity every child should have. With a few exceptions (see Exceptions to the Rules chapter), all children should be able to have a relationship with both parents. And often, you, the single mama, have to do everything in your power to make it happen. This can be extremely difficult when you are at odds with your children's father. But you have to put your kids' best interests before your bitter feelings.

It takes real maturity and a lot of prayer and loads of patience. By the time you've made up your mind to get rid of your children's father, you've probably lost respect for him. You may hate his guts. So how do you go about trying to involve this man in your child's life?

Deciding to do the right thing is not something you should expect to do right away. You do need time to get over the initial shock of your anger and hurt. At some point, however, you're going to have to look to a friend or a relative, another single mama who somehow has managed to have her single life without depriving her children of the opportunity to know their father.

Talking about your situation with other single parents, both mothers and fathers, is very healing. It also gives you a chance to hear from those with whom you're sharing. You'll learn how they set up visitation schedules. You'll discover that both parents can be at the same Little League game or school play without having a confrontation. You'll see that at some point, you or your ex will probably take another lover, and that the boyfriend or girlfriend may be in your children's life. Seeing these things in other relationships will soften the blow a little when the time comes for you to face these realities.

Many women know they're going to be single mamas even before their children are born. I'm not talking about single mamas by choice, either. I'm talking about women who were unlucky enough to get pregnant that one time they were careless about birth control. Okay, well, not necessarily the one time they were careless, just one of the times. They are women who really have no business with a particular man, because this man is not committed enough to her to even consider being there for her in her pregnancy, let alone after her baby's born.

These single mamas are challenged from day one about making a commitment to their children to allow them to know and love their fathers. Often these are men who otherwise wouldn't even be in their lives.

So you ask, why bother? Why not just let the guy get lost, if he chooses, and then concentrate on bringing up your child? Why go through all the trouble of trying to involve him in your child's life and vice versa? Plus, can't a stepfather be just as good?

Many children of single mamas grow up feeling abandoned. They ask a lot of questions about their father that their mother simply cannot answer, because she doesn't know.

Hangers-on

There's another group of single mamas on the other end of the spectrum when it comes to the father. These mamas refuse to accept the fact that Daddy does not want to make three. They mess up a perfectly good opportunity to allow their children to be involved in their mother's life and their father's life by making unsuccessful attempts to make it one life.

Often, especially when they first find themselves alone with their children, single mamas are so afraid, they cling to the hope that someday their children's father will come to his senses and return to the family.

Most women become single mothers when the fathers leave or die. In the latter case, there's often a desperate search for a replacement. This comes later for women whose men have fled. But usually the desperate search for what I call "male mend," (see chapter 4) starts with the biological father.

Some single mamas spend their entire lives hoping and praying their children's father will eventually become a permanent part of their lives. They often are in denial, allowing the father in and out of the family's life, pretending everything is fine. The children's father is often allowed to come and go as he pleases, despite the fact that he may have another family, or other women and other children elsewhere. This confuses the children and creates an insecure environment for the mother and her children. Children from these homes often repeat the cycle, thus creating generations of single-mama-headed households.

Once it becomes clear to you that the father has no intentions of being a part of your life, you are a single mama. There is nothing you can do to change that. Many women spend their children's entire childhood trying to get their baby's father to stick around.

Even after the child's grown up and has his own kids, these single mamas may be sharing their children's father with some other woman, and by now, other children. Get real and get a life. When the writing's on the wall, move on and just play with the cards you're dealt.

It is time for single mamas to break the cycle, to teach their children that, although single-mama-headed homes are not the healthiest of situations for Mom or the children, a single mama can survive. In order for a mother to communicate this to her child, she must first be convinced of it herself. She must stop chasing the dream and take on the task before her. She must do everything in her power to raise a well-balanced, self-assured child.

Your Kids Are Not Pawns

Your kids should never have to suffer from your decision not to be with their father. I know it is difficult to expect you to want to have a man in your life whom you find spineless, worthless, shameless, and hopeless. But, ladies, when you made the decision to sleep with this man, you took a chance. The consequences are those adorable children who deserve to love both their mother and their father despite what Mom and Dad feel for one another.

Often we single mamas try to be martyrs or heroes. We want to be everything to our children. We secretly want our kids to take our side. So we manipulate them from early on.

It usually starts with what we say to our kids behind their father's back. How many times have you told your young child about something his or her dad did to hurt you? How many times have you discussed his misdeeds with your girlfriends in your children's presence? Kids know when you're saying something bad about their father. Often they'll interrupt you or act out in some inappropriate fashion. They may do something to divert your attention. I've seen a lot of single mamas miss these cues because they're so preoccupied with their own agendas.

Babies as young as two years old will know when you're talking about their daddies. This is a way to start your child young on a course of having low self-esteem, of feeling worthless. It also forces the kids to make adult decisions that kids shouldn't have to make. It simply is not fair to put this kind of trip on a little person. If you love your kids, you'll want them to have every opportunity for success; forcing them to choose sides and manipulating them into having ambivalent feelings about their flesh and blood simply is not fair.

When I became a single mama, I had no idea how blessed I was to have learned some of my mistakes from girlfriends whom I'd observed. I'd watched them survive pregnancies all alone, and I'd shared in their early single mamahood.

Very often, once single mamas make up their minds to shake their addiction to their children's father, it's too late. We've already let our children see our hate for their father. We've aired too much of their father's dirty laundry and allowed the children to learn things about the relationship that they're far too young to understand.

Single mamas must be careful to protect their children's innocence. We must take extreme measures to keep our arguments away from the kids. There's no reason we have to discuss with our girlfriends in our children's presence why we cannot stand our ex. Kids begin to understand at a very young age when you're saying something negative about their father.

In my experience as a news reporter and a single mama, I've witnessed mothers taking all kinds of desperate measures to keep their children's father out of the kids' lives. Often these women have no idea they're doing these things out of spite. I've even seen women convince themselves that their child's father is abusing the kids. It has always baffled me that a woman who lives with a man never thinks of him as a pervert until after she catches him with another woman. Ladies, I'm here to say just because a man is a cheater does not mean he's a child predator. Before you go accusing your ex of doing inappropriate things to your kids, you'd better have proof, or you'll live to regret it. Who wants their children to grow up thinking they're related to a pervert? I'm not saying that if it's true, you shouldn't keep your kids as far away as possible. I'm just saying be careful; don't do it out of revenge.

So many African-American kids grow up feeling abandoned by their fathers and cheated by their mothers because of decisions we

Keeping the Anger Under Wraps

✽ Never argue with the father in front of the children.

✽ Write down any issues you have with the father to discuss when you're level headed.

✽ Never have angry telephone conversations with the father while the children are in earshot.

✽ Never say anything negative about the father in your children's presence.

✽ Be careful not to confide in mothers of your children's friends who might blabber to their kids.

✽ Be cordial to the father in your children's presence (and whenever possible when they are not around) and to any of his friends and family.

✽ Count silently to ten before opening your mouth whenever the father says something in your children's presence that angers you.

✽ When you have nothing good to say about the father to your children, say nothing at all.

✽ Invite the father to the kids' special events and programs.

✽ Speak first to any woman the father has with him when you see him.

✽ If your anger is too tough to control, get counseling.

single mamas make when we're hurt and angry. We set up ridiculous rules for our children's fathers, telling them they can't see the kids if they're going to have "that woman" or that B-word with them.

Some single mamas carry these rules with them into their next relationships, even their remarriages. If your ex tried to set those kinds of restrictions on you, you'd probably think he was crazy.

Well, you're just as crazy to do it to him. Believe me, doing this will deprive your child of the love he deserves.

You may not be able to stand the sight of your children's father, but the very image of your ex may be enough to cheer your kid up on a bad day at school. Give your children copies of old family photos to keep in their bedrooms. Make special scrapbooks for them to keep and share with their friends. Frame a favorite photo of each child with his father for him or her to keep in a special place.

From time to time, the kids will stare at these photos and ask you a lot of questions about what happened. Remind them that you split off with their dad because the two of you could not get along. Tell them the breakup had nothing to do with them, and that you both love them very much.

Keeping Communication Lines Open

Allow your kids to call their father on the telephone whenever they'd like. If it involves a long-distance call, set aside special times of the day when it's cheaper, and explain to the kids that the only reason you're limiting the calls is that long-distance calls during the workdays are very expensive.

If you have a computer and your ex is online, get your own online service and encourage the kids to spend time writing to their father. If not, encourage them to write the old-fashioned way and make stamps available.

Children are proud of their special relationships with their father. The communication will give them something to share with their friends when the subject of "my dad" comes up. It is bad enough that your children will not get to see their father every day. Do all that you can to make the relationship as rich as possible.

Plenty Love to Go Around

At some point, every single mama fantasizes about being part of a perfect family situation. Even if you end up with a man who loves your kids, remember that your children will want a relationship with their own father as well. A man in your life will not, and should not, replace your children's father. He should make their lives richer, adding one more person for them to love. Remember, love is not like a pie that can be cut into only so many pieces. In order for your child to love one person, he does not have to take love away from someone else.

Do not be threatened by your child's love for his father. If you let him love his dad and make it easy, your child will only love you more in the long run. In the near term, it will pay off in how your child relates to classmates, other adults, and you at home.

The more you leave your child's father out of his life, the more your child will suffer. If possible, invite your children's father to their special occasions, birthday parties, graduations, baptisms. It will foster a sense of "my parents may not be crazy about one another, but they love me." Put your ego aside for the sake of your children. Check your ego before you show your behind. Too many children's special events have been ruined by their single mama's funky attitudes.

Forget the issue of the other woman. In the end, she will not matter. Besides, if your ex was a dog with you, he's probably a dog with her, too. If you love your children, you can grin and bear the presence of some other woman (even the one who took your man) for long enough to see your child smile. A kid's smile from feeling the love of both parents goes a long way. It makes her confident. It gives her the courage to feel she can do anything. You want the best for your kids. Do not forget that. Your children's happiness and success is far more important than your pride.

I've heard from single fathers who say they would have spent more time with their children, but the kids' mothers made it nearly impossible. Although I think this is a lame excuse, there's some justice to it. If all a man needs is a lame excuse to go on with his life and hope his kids end up with a man who loves them and their mother, your selfishness will only make it easier for him to walk away. In the long run, the kids will suffer. Despite what other man ends up in their life, an emptiness will always be there.

Instead, do everything in your power to foster a good relationship between the kids and their father. They deserve to give love to both parents and receive it in return.

Little Is Better Than None

Sadly, some single mamas go out of their way to involve their children's fathers in the kids' lives, but these fathers have every excuse under the sun for why they can't do this and why they can't do that. Ironically, many of these dads do not pay child support either. Dads tell me it's hard not to want to see their kids if their money is helping to take care of them. In those instances where Dad refuses to keep to a schedule and chooses instead to drop by only when it's convenient for him, there's little a single mama can do. But don't even discourage a little bit of involvement. In my opinion, little is better than nothing. Just be sure, as tempting as it may be, and as right as you may be about how trifling this man is, not to put him down in the presence of his children. Keep it to yourself. If your kids ask you about it, if they insist on answers from you about why their dad doesn't keep his word or why he's not more involved, tell them to take it up with him, because you do not know.

In some cases where the fathers flee the scene, it is extremely difficult for women to encourage healthy father-kid relationships. These fathers may surface so few times throughout their children's lives, that their appearances can be counted on one or two hands. These cases require an extreme amount of maturity on the part of single mamas.

When your children's father is a runaway daddy, the temptation is to trash him, to tell your kids their daddy's no good. But you must rise above what comes naturally. It is your duty, your responsibility as a single mama, to be as honest as possible with your kids' father, without putting him down. Let your kids express their feelings about wishing their dad was there. Tell them the truth, that you wish he were there, too, but that you cannot control another person's behavior. Tell them that there are many reasons dads flee, but those reasons have nothing to do with them. Tell them parents have a lot of trouble, feel a lot of guilt sometimes, and those problems can keep them from seeing their kids more often. Tell the kids you know this isn't fair, but that they have the right to feel however they want about their dads. Usually, surprisingly, your children will choose to still love their fathers. Sometimes, however, they feel so ashamed of loving someone who doesn't show love in return, that they'll pretend to hate their fathers. Secretly they want their fathers' love.

Here again, tell your children that you've chosen to go on with your life. But share with them any good stories you can possibly come up with about their dads. Share a couple of pictures, and allow your kids to put them in a special place. You'll be surprised how many times the kids will pull the photos out just to look at them. Children who have absentee dads will not feel complete, but they'll feel a lot more whole if they're able to at least have a small piece of him.

Toya

Toya's college boyfriend had been her sweetheart since high school. I couldn't half blame her for being so crazy about the brother. He was fine—tall, with a slim build and smooth skin: one of those "the blacker the berry, the sweeter the juice" types. Anyway, girlfriend was crazy about her Dawson.

In the third month of her junior year, Toya learned she had even more on her plate than classes and sorority business. At first, she had no idea what was going on. All she knew was that she'd acquired a sudden craving for spinach and toast with grape jelly. Turns out Toya was pregnant with Dawson's child.

Toya was so sleep-deprived during her sorority pledge period, that she sometimes had no idea what day it was. She was completely off schedule with her birth control pills.

Toya eventually dropped out of college and moved back home. She had a boy and named him after his daddy. By the time her son was two, she'd found a decent job and an apartment. Dawson had not made a commitment to Toya, and he had no intention of marrying her. Still, Toya let him come in and out of her life and her apartment as he pleased. All it took was a few "I'm sorry's" and some good lovin', and she was his for the night.

Needless to say, Little Daws spent a lot of his childhood not quite knowing what was going on or what to expect. He'd seen his dad with his mom; then he'd see Daddy with other women. He wanted a real family, like the kind he saw on TV. Whenever he told Toya how he was feeling, she'd cry. He saw her cry a lot; it was confusing. He didn't know how to react to her or his father sometimes. When his dad would leave after a two- or three-day stay, he would see his mother crying. He'd tell his mother he didn't like her, which only made Toya cry even harder. Toya felt little Daws always took his anger out on her.

They say it takes a man to get a woman's mind off another man. In Toya's case, that man was her attorney. During an angry moment, after Toya had learned that Dawson had married a girlfriend he'd been swearing he was through with, she'd finally made up her mind to hire a lawyer to collect child support. By then Little Daws was five years old.

Toya's lawyer was a married man, a few years older than Toya, but he had the hots for her. He knew Dawson was the only man she ever had eyes or anything else for. And a challenge was more than this man could take. He would do anything to get this woman, to prove he could have any woman he wanted.

He was patient. He only moved when Toya said it was okay.

Toya was invited to most of Dawson's family's big events. This time, it was his cousin's wedding. Toya was looking good. She at least wanted to remind this fool of what he could have had. Her son was to spend the weekend with his dad.

When Little Daws saw Dawson, he ran up to him and jumped into his arms. Dawson kept a tight grip on his wife's hand but clutched his son. The three of them walked toward Toya. She waited for him to speak. He didn't. He just walked right past her, as if she were a stranger. Toya was hot.

Before she knew it, she was on the phone with Mr. Lover Boy attorney. "Serve him," Toya told him. "Today!"

At the meeting a couple of weeks later, in Toya's lawyer's office, Dawson showed up with his lawyer. They'd agreed to settle out of court. The judge had ordered Dawson to pay fifteen hundred dollars a month in child support for the next few years. It would be reduced after he became current. He also had to pay a separate check to Toya's lawyer for court costs. Dawson's attorney handed both checks over to the Lover Boy lawyer. And right there in front of

---

What Toya Could Have Done

* ✻ Collected child support from the get-go
* ✻ Made the choice early on to go on with her life, without chasing the dream that Daws would be there forever
* ✻ Realized there was no hope for Dawson and herself when he got married
* ✻ Let Daws have his relationship with his son, without jumping into bed with him
* ✻ Gotten support from a counselor or an objective friend
* ✻ Selected a lawyer who was a professional advocate instead of a man trying to take advantage of her
* ✻ Shown Little Daws consistent confident parenting
* ✻ Thought out her game plan instead of acting on an emotional whim
* ✻ Stuck to her guns

Dawson, Lover Boy, Esq., promptly handed both checks—the child support and his own fees—over to Toya.

Dawson could have died. For the first time in his life, he felt for sure he'd lost Toya to another man. No longer was his stuff the magic touch it had been. And he couldn't come close to matching up with his competition.

As soon as Dawson left with his lawyer, Toya jumped into Lover Boy's arms. They cleared that cherry wood table where this potentially life-changing event had taken place and made mad passionate love.

Toya bought a car and fixed up her apartment. When Dawson would come to see Little Daws, he'd stop at the front door, and he had nothing to say to Toya.

Time has a way of healing things, and as the months passed, Dawson started seeing his son more regularly, and he seemed to be getting over his anger toward Toya. Then Toya went back to some of her old ways.

She started letting Dawson sleep over from time to time, and she'd talk him into going on brief outings with her and Little Daws.

Little Daws has always had a strong relationship with his father. But kids learn by example. Little Daws learned it's okay for a man to have as many women as he wants. He learned it's okay for a woman to let a man have his way with her, despite the fact that he has never made a commitment to her.

Kelly

I was in the middle of frying tortillas for tacos when the phone rang. They were homemade tacos with deep-fried corn tortillas, ground beef flavored with salsa, grated sharp Cheddar cheese, chopped onions, tomatoes, and lettuce. They were my favorite meal then, and I made them at least once a week.

"Hi, Leon!" I said to my stepfather excitedly. "Oh, I'm fine; I'm making tacos."

Leon jokingly called me a Mexican and always teased me about my love for Mexican food. But he seemed happy to hear I was doing well and feeling happy. I'd been living in Wichita, Kansas, where I'd worked for the past year as a reporter at KSNW, channel 3. I was twenty-four with a master's degree and two and a half years' on-air TV reporting experience under my belt. Leon and my mother were proud of me. In a family of achievers, I was an overachiever, at least until now.

"It's great," I said. "I just bought a Tercel. You'd be so proud of how I negotiated that deal. Anyway, I'll pack my things and drive down there in a few weeks.

"No, Teddy's not coming. We just broke up. He's a dog. I'm not even taking his phone calls, Leon."

Leon was incredible. He was one of my best friends. He'd been married to my mother ever since I was a preteen. I trusted him more than any other single human being on earth. I could and did talk to him about everything. But he never said things that made me feel uncomfortable. It was always as if I was his biological daughter, and he respected my opinions, as well as whatever innocence I may have had. Perhaps it's because he's a doctor. I'm not sure. But he made it easy.

"Oh, I know. Christmas was fun. New York was incredible. I was there for New Year's, too."

Suddenly my mind wandered. I thought back to that beautiful New Year's Eve night. Teddy and I had taken a warm bubble bath together. Candles surrounded the tub. Jazz played in the background. We sipped champagne and made love all night long. And we promised one another it would be that way forever.

"But a week after I came back to Wichita, he was spending the weekend with some other woman. Anyway, I'm through with him. Other than that, everything else is good in my life. The new job, the new car. But there's just one thing, my health. I'm going to the doctor to find out what the problem is. My appetite's changed. I don't like eating the same foods. I just made these tacos, and I know you're not going to believe this, but I don't even feel like eating them. I'm nauseous all the time, and I just feel weird."

"Kelly, you sound like you're pregnant to me," Leon said matter-of-factly. "When was your last period? And aren't you using birth control?"

"You know I have irregular periods. And yes, I'm using a diaphragm. But come to think of it, I was at the end of my period the last time I did something. And I didn't use the diaphragm."

Leon knew. And the next day, I learned, too.

I walked into the Wichita office of Planned Parenthood with my mind cluttered. This was not the first time I was going to a clinic to get a pregnancy test. But for whatever reasons, this time I wasn't worried the way I was the other times. I didn't contemplate whether I could or would get an abortion. I didn't pray the test would come out negative. To this day, I'm not sure why, but I simply wasn't worried.

After I peed in the cup and gave the sample to the nurse, I sat in the waiting room as I was told. Several other young women came in after me for pregnancy tests. As the time passed, I sort of wondered why the nurse would call these teenage girls into another room, and why they all left before I did. But I didn't give that much thought either. The only possible explanation is that I was in a classic state of denial.

Finally. "Miss Williams, can you come with me, please?" I followed the nurse. Soon we were joined by another woman, a doctor. She introduced herself, and then, the verdict.

"Miss Williams, your pregnancy test has come back positive." The word "positive" seemed to echo. *"POSITIVE, positive, positive..."*

She followed up the declaration with information about other services, should I choose to terminate the pregnancy. On the way home, I felt a strange sort of peace. I smiled a little. The fear and shame would come days later. When it hit, it hit hard.

I called San Diego again to talk to my parents the next day. Leon was calm, almost expecting the news. Then he put my mother on the phone. She was devastated. The registered nurse in her came out immediately, as she took on a professional tone, advising me of my options. She was cold. How could this be? Her twenty-four-year-old daughter, for whom she had so many hopes and dreams, was now charting a fate that looked as unpromising as possible.

After I hung up the phone, I tortured myself with negative thoughts and fears. I, "Little Miss Straight A's" was pregnant. Here I was, my whole life ahead of me. My pregnancy made me feel that despite all my accomplishments, I'd let my family and myself down. And I was pregnant with no husband and a no-good ex-boyfriend whom I loved, but knew was a dog. Lord have mercy.

I thought back to Toya, about how I felt so sorry for her when I found out she had to drop out of school. At least this is happening to me now, I thought. I scanned my bedroom. On the wall were all my certificates of achievement. Both of my degrees, framed. Lincoln University, magna cum laude. Master's in journalism from the University of Missouri.

What in hell was I going to do? And whom was I fooling? Despite all the degrees, the real writing was on the wall. I was nothing more than a statistic. At least that's how I felt.

I put off talking to Teddy. I wasn't ready, and I didn't know what to say. I knew I wanted to have the baby, but I was certain he wasn't ready for a commitment. And I did not want to be a single mama.

What I Could Have Done

∗ Talked to a counselor or an objective friend

∗ Stopped feeling sorry for myself

∗ Talked to successful single mamas so I could realize getting pregnant when you're single does not mean you're doomed

∗ Understood that my mother was more disappointed in herself than she was in me

∗ Written a list of my assets—my education and work experience, family support

∗ Talked to Teddy openly and honestly about my feelings about the pregnancy

∗ Come up with a game plan

Alex

One day, I called my friend Alex to male-bash. Alex had been a single mama once, but now she was married to a wonderful man and, in addition to her son by her no-good ex-husband, she had a beautiful little girl.

We couldn't come up with a restaurant to meet for lunch, so she invited me to her place, where I made quiche and she made salad.

"My son's having such a tough time in school," she said. "And I know it's because of his terrible life. He has to spend two weekends out of the month with his father. Two toothbrushes, two combs, two pairs of pajamas. He has so much to keep up with, so much he has to be responsible for. I feel sorry for him."

This was the first time Alex had been so open with me about her situation. I never knew she was so angry with her ex. They'd been divorced for three years and her new husband, Ray, was a wonderful man who adored her and her son, Ryan. Ray and Alex also had a two-year-old daughter, Rashawna.

But today Alex was angry. All she could talk about was Ryan. Ryan

---

What Alex Could Have Done

✳ Gotten counseling before she remarried

✳ Stopped projecting her negative feelings on her son

✳ Worked on her healing, being honest about her feelings

✳ "Talked up" the two toothbrushes, combs, etc., as a positive, instead of making it a problem

✳ Moved forward in her life instead of living in the past

---

was seven, and he had been acting out in school. Alex blamed it on her ex-husband and his wife. She couldn't point to anything they had done wrong, but to Alex, if her husband had never left her for this woman he married, none of this would be happening.

"I can't stand that bitch," Alex told me.

"Did she exist when you did?"

"Yes. She was his mistress, his white mistress." Alex told me the only reason Ryan visited his dad and stepmom was that the visitations were strictly court enforced. She said for the first months of their separation, she fought any attempts by her ex to see their son. She was angry and thought no man who left his wife for another woman deserved to see his kid.

It's strange how much more easily you can see someone else's faults than you can see your own. It was clear to me right away that a lot of Ryan's so-called problems had to do with Alex's attitude. It was clear to me that she did not hesitate to express all these negative feelings in front of Ryan, his dad, and her new husband.

I suggested that she might want to look at Ryan's relationship with his dad as something exciting and fun instead of something burdensome. I told her that would probably make the visits less stressful. I even went so far as to suggest that her stresses about the whole situation were causing her son to become anxious. Alex would simply talk over me; she wasn't hearing it. However, she unknowingly was teaching me what I did not want to do with my son.

Tia and Kyle

Tia and her ex once owned a video dating service, of all things. Their marriage only lasted three years, but that was long enough for the couple to have two beautiful children. Money was always a problem for Tia and Kyle, until Kyle's parents died and he inherited an insurance policy and the family home. Kyle promised Tia he'd sell his parents' house and build her one of her own. She looked forward to this, since she'd always wanted to feel like a princess in a castle.

Tia was extraordinarily beautiful. She was petite, and always wore stylish, sexy clothing that flattered her waiflike figure. Kyle was short, about the same height as Tia, and was also good looking. Tia always found him attractive and interesting, but she'd confide in her friends that she felt Kyle wasn't quite good enough for her. She wanted an older man with money.

While Kyle was shopping around for land for their new house, Tia came to the realization that she just didn't love him. Even though she had two children, she wanted more out of the marriage. It wasn't fulfilling to her. Kyle loved Tia, and he tried to convince her she was making a terrible mistake. Soon the frustration and rejection got the better of him, and he started smoking crack cocaine; he eventually got arrested for possession.

Instead of feeling sorry for Kyle, Tia wanted out more than ever now, and she filed for a divorce. She also wanted full custody of the children.

Kyle moved out of the small apartment, humiliated. He wanted his wife back; he also wanted the kids. Kyle's biggest fear was that Tia had been seeing another man. Actually, she was dating an older and richer man she'd met through the dating service. She knew there was no way she and Kyle were going to make it. He just wasn't her type anymore.

Tia made all the classic mistakes in the beginning of the split-up. She'd get into shouting matches with Kyle when the children were

Don't Rebound

This, I know, is easier said than done, especially when you're feeling vulnerable. So often, people start a relationship before wrapping up the last one. This is particularly dangerous for the soon-to-be single mama.

It's easy to feel you're in love when a wonderful man is paying so much attention to you. But when you have children, their feelings come first. Do not get involved with someone new until you've resolved your anger and the financial situation with your ex. If this seems impossible, talk to a counselor. Or at least speed up your divorce.

present. She tried to demonize him, convincing herself and everyone else in her life that he was a total loser. Worse, she flaunted her new boyfriend in front of Kyle, positioning him as the kids' stepdad.

Tia was driving herself nuts. She felt she was on a treadmill when it came to her dealings with Kyle and the divorce. She was moving but getting nowhere. Her kids were a wreck. Her girl was really still a baby, not quite two years old. The boy was barely three. Still, they'd return from visits with their dad repeating curse words they'd heard him say. They were extremely clingy to their mother. Once her son said, "Daddy's a bad man." Both kids would throw huge fits whenever they had to separate from her. Tia could not see that her behavior had anything to do with it.

When Tia would talk to me about her problems, I'd just listen. She was not open to any preaching, so I laid off, at first. Then I started suggesting she be a little kinder to Kyle. I told her not to look at him as such a bad guy; instead, I told her to look at him as a wounded animal. He felt rejected and now was afraid he was losing his children. He knew he'd lost her. I told her that whenever Kyle did what he was supposed to do, thank him. Tell him she appreciated getting the child support on time. I suggested she thank him for simple things, like feeding the kids or washing their clothes before he returned them to her. I suggested Tia stop saying bad things about Kyle in front of the kids.

I really wanted to lecture Tia about how it was probably a little early in her relationship with the older man to be spending so much time with him away from the kids. I felt they needed her more now than ever. Yet she was infatuated, and her new guy was an escape. He'd take her on fabulous dinner dates and weekend getaways. He'd also sleep in her house with the kids there.

Tia never asked me about how I felt about the new relationship, so I didn't offer an opinion. Besides, I'd seen it before. I knew that getting into other relationships before the one with your children's father is resolved only serves to slow progress.

Marie and Casey

Marie's baby's daddy came by often when Casey was an infant an a toddler. But mostly it was to see what he could get from the baby's mama. Marie was willing to give this man anything he pleased, because she thought he'd see the light someday and marry her and give her a real family.

A few years passed, and finally it became clear to Marie that Casey had no intention of marrying her. She also realized he was not coming around to see his son, only to spend time with her. At the same time, this man had another girlfriend he'd been seeing all along. Eventually they got married.

Still, like so many single mamas, Marie would use her womanhood and her son to try to get her ex to keep her warm on lonely nights. She was in denial about his wife and later the children he'd had with her.

As Casey grew older, he'd ask about his father. He wanted to know why he didn't come around as much as he used to. Marie would encourage him to call his dad, and he would show up occasionally, to take Casey to Burger King or on some other token outing. Fortunately Marie had pretty much gotten over Casey's dad by then, so she never stood in the way of her son's attempts to involve his dad in his life.

As Casey grew in his preteen and teen years, Marie made sure he was involved in church groups and other activities that allowed him to have close relationships with responsible men. He always seemed to be trying to shop for a partner for his mama. Casey would often point to a man at church and say, "There's a man for you, Mama." Marie saw right through it. She knew he was actually shopping for a man to complete his own life.

One of Casey's biggest disappointments with his father came when he needed money for a tuxedo for his junior prom. Since Casey had a job at a fast food restaurant, he didn't need the whole amount and only asked for fifty dollars. His dad told him it would be no problem. In fact, he offered to give Casey fifty dollars more.

Casey, of course, was ecstatic. By the day of the prom, however, his father hadn't shown up with the money. Casey had already purchased his tux and the tickets, but he needed some extra cash to take his date out to dinner that night. Casey figured his dad would surprise him and show up just before he left so he could see his son in the tux. But just in case, Casey paged his dad that morning.

His father called back from out of town. He'd forgotten all about Casey and the junior prom. He spoke to Marie and asked her to loan their son the money. She gave Casey one hundred dollars, telling him it was from his daddy. It's been a year, and Casey's father has yet to pay Marie back, and just as she never pursued child support from this man, Marie hasn't pressed this issue either.

A week later, Casey was washing clothes at home and the machine broke. The clothing was clean and rinsed, but still soaked. Casey put the wet clothing in the dryer and called his mom at work to tell her the washer and dryer were both broken. Marie arrived home to find her dryer flooded with water.

Of course, Marie was so angry that she yelled at Casey, asking him how he could do something so stupid. Casey yelled back. Marie began pounding on Casey's chest. He told her he was too old for her to beat him, and he punched a hole in the wall of the house.

Later, when Casey and Marie talked about what had happened, they discovered that at the bottom of Casey's mistake were feelings of inadequacy, and at the bottom of Marie's anger was the incident with Casey's dad. Both of them were disappointed that he had disappointed Casey.

If You're in Marie's Shoes

✻ Constantly talk to your children, reassuring them when they feel unloved and insecure.

✻ Remind them regularly that their father's choices have everything to do with him and his problems and nothing to do with them.

✻ Go out of your way to involve your brothers, male cousins, or friends in your children's lives.

✻ Let your children know that your boyfriend will never replace their father.

✻ If necessary, get counseling for your children.

✻ Once your children are able to understand that their father's irresponsibility is not their fault, help them figure out how to always have a Plan B.

They realized there was nothing they could do to force Casey's dad to keep his word. But they agreed to talk about their feelings the next time, and they said they'd try not to take them out on one another.

2

Choices

Single mamas are usually antiabortion—at least we are when it comes to ourselves and our unborn babies. Think about all the times during your pregnancy or pregnancies that people talked to you about abortion. It was not an option for you. If you did consider it, even for a moment, you couldn't go through with it. If you were single when you became pregnant, you knew you were in a tough spot, but you decided somehow you'd deal with the pregnancy.

My mother, a retired school nurse, told me she noticed that with few exceptions at her junior high school, white girls handled their pregnancies differently than did African-American girls. Of course her study of the behaviors of pregnant teens was by no means scientific. It was based largely on the numbers of girls who confided in her about their pregnancies. She told me, "White girls have abortions; black girls have babies."

I've spoken to many young moms about their choice to have the child and much of it has to do with tradition and religion. Girls whose mothers were teen moms often handle their own pregnancies the way their moms did. I've talked to a number of single mamas who have had abortions, even used them as a means of birth control, before they finally felt so guilty that they decided to keep their child. In many black communities, however, abortion is still viewed as deeply wrong.

Many African-American girls do give up their children for adoption. But doing so is not typical in African-American communities. Black women know that the foster care system is overloaded with minority children. Ours are not the children so many wonderful childless couples are eager to adopt. They're looked at as "special needs" kids. We'd rather do what we can to take care of our own kids than to live with the guilt of wondering whether our children are languishing in foster care.

Diane

Every year, Diane dreaded two dates, one in October, the other in December. They were the due dates of the babies she never had. She'd had two abortions, both conceptions from sex with the same married man.

Both times, Diane had cried day and night for weeks. She couldn't bear revealing to her family that she was having an affair with a married man. Nor would she risk losing this man she loved so dearly. She knew he did not want her to have a child. Diane couldn't imagine bringing a child into the world who would grow up knowing how immoral his or her mother had been, sleeping with a married man. So as difficult as the decision was, she made it twice—and so had two abortions. Her choice caused her a lot of shame and pain. Diane could not and would not forgive herself. Lying there on the table after her second abortion, she vowed never to get another one. No matter what the circumstances, she would keep her baby the next time she got pregnant.

Diane's first pregnancy was really her own fault. She took too many chances, having sex without birth control. The second time caught her by surprise. She'd just started taking a low-dosage birth control pill. After she got pregnant, her doctor told her she should have been using an alternative form of birth control along with the pill during her first month on it. Not knowing this, she ended up being one of a fraction of birth-control pill users who gets pregnant on the pill.

Several years after Diane and her married man finally broke up for good, she found herself involved with a decent single guy. Diane

What Diane Did Right

* Listened to her heart and stayed focused on doing single mamahood right
* Came up with a serious plan
* Got counseling
* Suggested Frank get involved in counseling
* Read books on parenting in two homes
* Made parenting her priority, rather than making Frank her priority
* Got her child's financial and family life in order early

was thirty-five, and she had been dating Frank only a few months when she learned she was pregnant. Once again, she was taking that low-dosage pill. Only this time, she had been taking it longer than a month, but her doctor claimed the problem was she wasn't taking the pill at the same time every day. To Diane, her pregnancy was a sign from God that it was time for her to be a mother. She'd already "gotten rid" of two babies; she was not going to have another abortion.

Frank tried to talk to Diane about all their options. When he mentioned abortion, Diane was adamantly against it. She told Frank she was not trying to trap him, that in fact she did not expect him or want him to marry her. She told him she would like to continue dating him, and she hoped he would be a supportive father. She had no expectations beyond that.

Diane had a good job as a department store manager, her health benefits were excellent, and she had no worries about taking care of this child. Her parents were not especially excited about her decision, nor was her sister. But Diane would not hear any more talk about abortion. She'd been there, and she wasn't going to do it again. This time, she was going to do the right thing and have her baby.

Diane had been to counseling before (it's how she had been able to get out of the relationship with the married man) and she knew she needed it this time, too. She suggested that Frank go with her, and he agreed. They also bought books on how to share custody, and even before Diane was six months pregnant, they had a schedule for child support and visitation. Diane was fortunate. It turns out Frank's mind was so eased by Diane's honesty and by the fact that she was not trying to "trap" him, that he, too, was excited about having a child, even if it wasn't under the most ideal conditions.

Frank was there when Diane had their little boy. He was there for his beautiful son throughout his first two years. He grew much closer to Diane and her parents. Outsiders marveled at what an incredible father he was. Diane grew to love Frank, and he grew to love her, and by their son's third birthday, Diane and Frank had married. Their son was the ring bearer in the wedding.

Resources if You're in Diane's Shoes

* Family
* Churches
* Single mama friends
* Support groups
* Family therapists
* Single mothers' shelters

3

The "Male Mend"

A single mama-to-be is one of the most vulnerable creatures on earth: She's caught between feelings of regret and hope. Most single mamas, if they're honest, will tell you they don't want to be single, but that things just worked out that way. Sometimes their feelings of desperation lead them to making some unwise choices.

When single mamas are afraid, the first thing they often think about is the "male mend." Having a man instantly gives you hope of changing your status. It makes you feel that during the time that he's in your life you're not a single mama. If you're lucky, you choose a man who likes children and who loves your kids. He likes to do things with them, and he helps you out.

While you're kissing frogs, though, to find this Prince Charming, you often find yourself in some hopeless situations. You run the risk of rushing to the altar, thus complicating your children's lives further.

Ladies, please do not rush to get married. A man will not solve your problems; in fact sometimes, he'll compound them. Often a man becomes another responsibility altogether. He's an extra mouth to feed, another set of feelings not to hurt, and someone who must fit into your unique family. His very presence will change the dynamics of your life.

I'm not saying there's something necessarily wrong with that. I do believe, however, a man must be worth it for you to make that kind of sacrifice. Ask yourself, "What is this man doing for me?" The answer does not have to be that he's providing some kind of financial support in order for you to decide he's worth it. In fact, a man who solves all your financial problems often comes at a high price. He can cost you your independence, your sense of self, and your children's affection.

For a man to be worth it, he should provide you some emotional support. He should allow you to be yourself, and you should feel free to be the kind of mother you want to be. If you have to alter your personality around a man, there's a problem. Ask yourself—is it really worth it? Is he worth it? What will this do to my kids? Is it in their best interest? Don't make another mistake.

I am not boyfriend-bashing, but single mamas are so vulnerable when it comes to men. We often want what most single women want: a husband. And we want what any mother wants: a father for our children. Many people who love us feel sorry for us. In church, people pray that we'll find a husband and a father for our kids. In the beginning, it's almost second nature to size up every man we go out with as a prospective husband, because, quite frankly, we don't have a whole lot of time to be kissing frogs.

But, ladies, it ain't that easy. Single mamahood is so complicated. Our children's needs are special, and so are ours. We have to be very careful when it comes to finding that right man or we can make a bad situation worse.

Although, technically, single mamas who "male mend" their relationships are not really single, I've chosen to include them in the book. In many ways, these mothers are still single mamas who just went through the motions, or they've started their new lives without considering what impact their new life will have on their children.

Stepfamilies can work. I know that firsthand, because it worked for my mother and her four children and Leon and his three. But there were some serious adjustments that had to be made in those early years in order for things to go smoothly. I think single mamas should consider the impact of their decision to get married before they go to the altar.

I think women who remarry before they learn how to be successful single mamas bring a lot of extra baggage into their children's lives. These women are so concerned about everyone else's impressions of how their family looks on the outside, that the inside is toxic. It's like a hamburger that looks fully cooked, but it's full of bacteria.

Usually this kind of situation arises through no real fault of the single mama. After all, she simply wants peace in her life and stability for her children. Often a new man offers these things, at least initially.

This is not to male bash. Single mamas make this mistake with perfectly good men as well as with the losers. In fact, I have two extremely good friends who have married terrific guys who are now excellent stepfathers and role models for their children. The only problem is that both of my friends have lived their lives as though their children's biological fathers did not exist. In the end, the kids were affected by the loss.

Before you decide to bring another man into the picture, explore with your child his or her feelings about the matter. Do not say that your son or daughter is getting a new daddy; instead say that you're getting yourself a new husband. If the children choose, after a time, to love this man as a father, that's the kids' business. I think children will naturally learn to love a decent man. I know my brothers and sisters and I learned to love Leon. But do not force the love you have for this man on your kids. Neither should you pretend your fiancé is the fix to all your family problems. It will set your man up for a big fall. Eventually your kids, no matter how much they love this man, will long for their own father. They'll feel rejected, and often they'll blame you.

Salena

Salena lived on the north side of Jacksonville, Florida, in the heart of the 'hood. She had been divorced about a year and a half. Her two sons, Chris and Charles, lived with her. Chris was a couple years older than my son, Winston, and Charles was a year younger. A friend of Salena's who worked with me invited me to a party that Salena and her boyfriend, Sam, were hosting.

Later Salena and I became friends, and I learned more about her relationship with Sam. Salena looked at Sam as the man who would rescue her from the poverty her ex-husband had left her in. Her ex was an engineer by profession, but he had quit a steady job to become an entrepreneur. That left her, during their marriage, to carry the financial weight of the relationship. After they divorced, her ex refused to pay child support.

Salena was a college-educated woman on the fast track, working as a sales rep for a computer firm. Sam was not college educated, but he made a good income as a finance company manager. He spent a lot of time explaining why he did not need a college degree to be successful, appearing, in my opinion, to be threatened by his girlfriend's educational achievements.

Sam was good with his hands; in fact, that was one of the things Salena liked about him. He'd fix everything that broke in her little house in the 'hood. He even helped her remodel it a little. But he was an old-school disciplinarian. Unlike Salena, he believed children should be seen and not heard. He'd often raise his voice with the kids and get into long debates with Salena, accusing her of having no idea how to bring up two black boys.

Salena would discuss with me Sam's feelings about her parenting skills, and she'd often share her concerns about raising two boys without a father. The boys would visit their father whenever possible, but Salena thought they needed a father figure in their lives on a daily basis.

Salena and I would take turns helping each other babysit. I'd keep her two boys some nights, and she'd keep Winston for me other nights. When we went out together, my babysitter would keep all the kids, or Salena's mother would watch them all. We had a nice system going.

Often Salena would call me or hook up with me to vent about Sam.

"Girl, I don't know what I'm going to do about this man," she'd say. "He is so good to me and the boys. He takes me out to dinner, buys us groceries, he's always there when I need him. And, girl, he is such a great lover. But sometimes he's so controlling, it gets on my last nerve."

What Salena Could Have Done

* Received counseling to resolve her feelings of insecurity and desperation
* Talked to women who'd remarried to get a feel for the kinds of issues she might confront
* Taken her time before jumping from the frying pan into the fire
* Worked with Consumer Credit Counseling to set up a realistic budget, without relying on a man's financial support

"What do you mean, 'controlling'?"

"Well, you know, he's always trying to tell me how to discipline the boys. He thinks I baby them. And he's really into this beating thing, always telling me I spare the rod too much."

"How do you feel about that?"

"I don't know, maybe he's right. But he comes from one of those huge families. He was raised in the country, and I just think he doesn't get the fact that things have changed.

"I think I was doing fine with Charles and Chris before Sam came along. But I do think they need a male figure in their lives. I really don't know that much about raising boys. In my family, it was just me and my sister."

It seems Salena and I had that conversation a dozen times over the course of the next year. That's why I was disappointed, but not surprised, when she told me she and Sam were getting married. I knew Salena loved Sam, but I thought she was rushing to fix what she viewed as her broken family.

Within four months of the marriage, Salena began to see Sam's insecurities in a whole new light. He was hard on her boys. He seemed to still have a relationship with his ex-wife that went beyond dealing with their children (there were three). Salena told me sometimes Sam would get verbally abusive with her and the kids.

Resources for Women in Crisis

* Abuse hotlines
* Support groups for abused women
* Shelters for abused women
* Churches
* Friends and family
* Hospital emergency rooms

One day, a couple years after they married, Salena learned that Sam hadn't been paying their mortgage (his only financial obligation to his new family), and they were evicted. Salena seemed to have gone from bad to worse in a short period of time just because friends, society, and members of her church had convinced her that her boys needed a father and she needed a husband.

A few months after the eviction, Salena called me in tears. She was at her mother's house. She had left Sam. She said he had been verbally and physically abusive. Fortunately her boys were visiting their father for the summer and missed the drama. She wanted to be sure it stayed that way. So when the boys returned, it was to Grandma's house, not Sam's. They'd been back four days, and neither had asked about Sam. By the end of that year, Salena was a single mama again, starting all over once more.

Petricia

When I met Petricia, she had been married to Blevins for less than a year. She had a fourteen-year-old son named Kenny, who was the quietest teenager I'd ever met. The boy lived in his bedroom, and the funk that hit you in the face when you opened the door was overwhelming. It smelled like a boy's room, but a hundred times worse. It seemed Kenny only left that room to eat and to use the bathroom—and I'm sure he never stepped into the shower while he was there.

Tension in Petricia's house was about as thick as the funk in

Kenny's bedroom. Petricia, a purchaser for a big pharmaceutical company, was a very outgoing woman, and she was always thinking of ways to make money on her own. She'd been talking a lot about starting a networking group for single African-American professionals in St. Petersburg. It would be a local chapter of a national networking group that had already begun to take shape and become quite popular among upwardly mobile African Americans in other cities throughout the country. Blevins seemed to support all of Petricia's entrepreneurial ventures. Clothing from a boutique she'd opened and had to close hung in the garage, and, apparently, the two of them had worked on a couple of other failed projects together. But Blevins never tired to talk Petricia out of her dreams.

Blevins was a pleasant guy who didn't seem to get upset or emotional about anything. But whenever Kenny ventured from his hellhole, you could see the disdain on Blevins's face. His whole mood changed.

One night I finally mustered the courage to ask Petricia about Blevins and Kenny. "How well do Kenny and Blevins get along?" I asked, faking innocence.

"Not at all," Petricia answered with a chuckle. "Blevins has never liked Kenny, and Kenny's never liked him. Blevins thinks Kenny's a big baby. He always tells me I spoil him and that he should do more work around the house. He thinks Kenny's lazy."

"What do you think?" I asked.

"I think he's just a kid. He's a real good kid. He's always been a real independent kid. When Blevins and I were dating, he'd stay home by himself, fix his own food, everything, and he never complained."

"How old was he?" I asked.

"Oh, about five or six."

"Five or six!" I exclaimed. "You let him stay by himself when he was that young?"

"Oh yeah," she answered cavalierly.

I thought she was either stretching the truth to let me know how mature Kenny was, or she was crazy. But I liked Petricia too much to get self-righteous on her.

"What kind of food did he fix?"

"Whatever was in the house. Bologna, chips, cupcakes—stuff like that."

"So when did Blevins start having a problem with him?"

"Always has. Kenny's just always kept to himself when Blevins is around."

"Did you talk to Kenny about your plans to marry Blevins before you did it?"

"Not really. I just pretty much told him we were getting married."

"How 'bout Kenny's dad, do they communicate?"

"Oh no. He was very abusive. I married Kenny's dad when I was a teenager, and he was much older. I got away from him because he was so abusive. Kenny doesn't even know him."

After a few months, Petricia and Blevins split up. Petricia and I have since spoken more candidly. She told me the breakup had everything to do with the relationship Blevins and Kenny did not have. To this day, Kenny is still very introverted; he still lives with his mama and rarely ventures outside of his bedroom. He recently finished high school, and soon he's supposed to enroll in some junior college courses. But he pretty much just works his job at a fast-food restaurant and comes home to watch TV in his bedroom.

I often wondered whether Petricia was in denial about the fact that her son did not have any relationships. I wondered how much of what appeared to be highly dysfunctional behavior had to do with Kenny's relationship or lack thereof with his mother. I know teenagers rarely do a lot of sharing of their feelings and experiences with their parents, but there seemed to be absolutely no interaction between Kenny and his mom. I wondered if, perhaps, Petricia's drive to be a successful entrepreneur was more important to her than seeing to it that her son grew up to be a contributing member of society. I wonder if her inability to assign him chores and her acceptance of his hermitlike behavior kept him from having a healthy relationship with the only man who ever showed any interest in him. It was almost as though Kenny wasn't really there. I never saw any parenting displayed by Petricia, good or bad. It seemed no one, not her husband, nor myself, could get her to see that something was wrong with the way she was bringing up her son.

What Petricia Could Have Done

* Taken parenting classes when Kenny was young
* Gotten Kenny involved with sports and other extracurricular activities
* Hired a babysitter who had other children
* Tried to put Kenny on a visitation schedule with his dad (who, by the way, was never abusive to Kenny)
* Allowed Blevins to spend time alone with Kenny before she got married
* Talked to Blevins about how he saw his relationship with Kenny
* Allowed Kenny to share his feelings about Blevins, or anything for that matter
* Snapped out of denial and brought in a family counselor

Kevin

Kevin thought he would die when his mother told him she was marrying Reverend Jones. He was stunned. First of all, he never liked the guy; he always noticed Reverend Jones staring at his mother during church services. Kevin knew his mother didn't get so much religion all of a sudden that she had to go to church three times every Sunday. He knew the only reason he had to be in that hot church all day had something to do with Reverend Jones, so he just didn't like him.

Later, the good Reverend started coming to their house for Sunday dinner. His mother would go all out—she'd even put candles on the table. Kevin wondered why she never lit candles when she cooked dinner for him.

Things really got out of hand in a few months, when Kevin's mother told him he couldn't sleep in her bed anymore. Even though Kevin was twelve and didn't fall asleep there that often anymore, he liked that king-size bed. The idea that his mother would stay up late and watch TV with the Reverend with the door closed was enough to make Kevin want to vomit.

Kevin liked being the man of the house. His mother never made any major decisions without getting his input. She asked him what color carpet she should put in the den; she let him decide what she should cook for big dinners; she let him go with her to pick out new appliances or furniture.

Kevin even liked doing chores around the house. He was proud of the fact that his mother never had to ask him to put out the garbage or to return the can to the backyard after the garbage man came. He was proud when his mother would come home after working on a Saturday to find the lawn mowed or the hedges trimmed. Kevin was his mother's little man. He liked that.

But things changed when the Reverend started hanging around the house. Kevin thought he'd lose it one Monday morning when he got up early to put the trash can in the front yard only to find Reverend Jones had already put it out. Not only that, his car was still parked in the driveway. When Kevin asked his mother about it, she just told Kevin not to worry, that Reverend Jones wanted to take care of the chores, and that was okay with her. Kevin was completely left out when his mother let Reverend Jones decide what would be on the menu that next Sunday. Over the next few months, Kevin's opinion didn't seem to count anymore.

Kevin was not surprised when his mother told him she and Reverend Jones were getting married. Of course, Kevin didn't even have a chance to get his two cents in about his feelings in the matter. Kevin's mother never asked him how he felt. She just said that from then on, Kevin would no longer be the man of the house.

Kevin felt himself withdrawing from his family; it was a family he no longer recognized. He started spending a lot more time with his friends—and some of his friends changed. There were tougher boys who'd let him do things that made him feel bigger and stronger. They'd even let him drink beer and wine with them. Kevin's grades started slipping; he began to skip school.

Kevin's mother was taken aback by her son's behavior. She just couldn't believe what was happening. She had no idea how she'd gone wrong. All her single-mama life, people had been telling her

---

Don't Forget the Kids

When you find someone special, let your children know what's going on. Consider their feelings at all times. Take notice of what's happening with their emotions and behavior.

If your relationship is taking a toll on your children, back up. Take your time. Get help for the kids, and yourself, if necessary. Do not invite a new person into the family until everyone's ready.

Your children's father can be a valuable resource during these difficult times.

---

she'd better hurry up and get married, that her son needed a man in the house. Yet, just when she found one, Kevin started to change. He'd always been such a good boy until then.

Kevin's mother asked her husband to talk to his stepson. He did, but of course he couldn't get through to Kevin. Reverend Jones was confused and felt inadequate when it came to dealing with Kevin. He'd really never had too many dealings with him outside of church.

That summer, Kevin went to his father's house out of state. He talked to his dad about how he was feeling. His dad said it was natural. He explained that Kevin's mother had no intention of hurting him, that she probably thought she was helping him. He told his son to enjoy being a kid. He said it was good that Kevin didn't have so much responsibility anymore, and he told him to try not to grow up so fast, that he'd have plenty of time to be a man.

Kevin ended up doing well in high school, and he even went to college. He struggled in his own marriage later. He's now a single dad. He does all he can to be there when his kids need him. He knows it can make all the difference in the world.

4

Help!

The transition between being with your children's daddy and being without him is the toughest time in the life of a single mama. You're often confused, hurt, and angry at the same time. You're filled with love for your children and hatred for their father. Yet, as you battle your emotions, you're being forced to make difficult decisions.

During this time, you need help. You need your family and you need some kind of objective support, someone who will not take sides. You need to be in a support group for other single mamas and you might need counseling.

If your employer has an employee assistance program (EAP), use it. Ask around at your church and in your girlfriend group about low-cost mental health services. When you have a bad cough or an aching back, you don't ignore it, so don't ignore your heartache either. You need healing for your children and for yourself.

The worst thing you can do is deny you have "issues." Don't fool yourself into thinking you have everything under control. Watch your children's behaviors. Are they crying more than usual? Are you getting calls from their teachers? Are they fighting among themselves more? If so, they are as hurt as you are. The only way you'll really know whether you're handling this transition properly is to get the opinion of a third party.

How We View Counseling

Often African-Americans view counseling as something that's just for white folks who are messed up in the head. We think of counselors as "shrinks." "I'm not telling that woman all my business!" How many times have you heard that?

A counselor can be someone from your church or a community group. Your best bet when you're breaking up with your man and there are children involved, is to deal with someone who is experienced in handling your kind of situation. Try not to go to someone who will take sides. You can get that for free from one of your family members. Honestly, it won't do you much good in the long run either.

For me, counseling had an incredible impact. This is not to say some good old-fashioned common sense from older sisters and "sistas" will hurt; it's just that you need an objective opinion to weigh in with all the other advice. My point is you need advice from someone wiser than yourself.

Help From Loved Ones

Talk to people who love you, and those who care about you but aren't so close to you. It won't hurt to talk to someone who cares both about you and about your children's father.

During this time, you'll be self-righteous and won't want to hear what half the people coming to you with advice will have to say. Instead of weighing the advice, consider the source. If the person offering support is someone who in the past has shown concern for your well-being, take her advice seriously now. Consider the age of the person as well. If older women have something to say to you, nine times out of ten it's probably worth hearing.

What you need right now, whether you want to accept it or not, is help. You need advice and you need direction. Listen to the older ladies in your family and circle of friends, because chances are they know what they're talking about.

Unfortunately you'll have to learn how to tell the difference between healthy and unhealthy advice. A lot of people will be offering you the kind of support you want, but that you don't necessarily need. Sometimes, women who are unhappy themselves as single mamas will offer you bad advice. They'll suggest you hold a grudge against your ex or that you discourage your children from being with their father if he's with a new girlfriend. This will sound good, but it is not sound advice. Remember, misery loves company. A healthy single mama must break the mold. She must be different from all those single mamas who hang on to the hope that their ex will come back to the family or that he'll have a change of heart someday and decide he really loves his children's mother. A healthy single mama gets on with her life and learns to let go of the pain and hostility. She rebuilds what she has, using what's available, not what she hopes she'll have someday.

Do not discount professional help. It will pay off in the present and the future. Only with the help of an objective third party will you be able to see who your real friends are and which single mamas really have their heads screwed on straight.

Girlfriends and "Group"

I always thought Darlene had her stuff together. She was a single mama herself who always looked like a million bucks at work. She wore braided extensions in sophisticated styles and her clothes always flattered her sista' girl figure, which was tall and shapely, especially on the backside. And she had a mean set of legs that she played to the hilt.

Darlene always wore three-inch heels and skin-tight skirts. A couple of them were leather. I'd often tease her and say she was our "sex-ta-tery." But Darlene was no black blonde. She'd completed at least some college and was a master with the language. She often helped the managers craft press releases and speeches we'd write. But no one topped this East St. Louis girl when it came to street smarts, especially when the subject was men.

I met Darlene when Winston was a year old. Teddy and I had moved to Los Angeles, married, and were well on our way to divorce.

Darlene and I were like two old ladies when we got together. We'd brag about our cooking skills. Holidays were the worst. We'd be on the phone bragging about our homemade cornbread dressing, candied yams, and pecan pies.

Darlene often talked to me about her six-year-old daughter, Carmen. Darlene called her Li'l Bit. Li'l Bit was Darlene's heart and soul. She sent her to a private school and made sure that little girl had high self-esteem. Darlene was real good about making sure Li'l Bit spent time with her father. She was the first single mama I'd met who knew how to put her own problems with her ex aside for the sake of her child.

Darlene's sixth sense kicked right into gear the first time she met Teddy. Even when he was fooling me, he did not fool Darlene. From time to time, I would confide in Darlene. She would tell me similar stories about her ex. To me, it was amazing how she and this man she once hated cooperated when it came to Li'l Bit. Darlene would go to him when she needed extra cash. The two of them worked together when it came to sharing responsibilities involving Li'l Bit, and Darlene didn't mind if her ex had a girlfriend with him when he picked his daughter up from her home. Nor did he mind that Darlene had a guy over when he arrived. I had no idea, then, but I had a lot to learn from Darlene.

One day I told her I honestly did not know whether Teddy had been screwing around, but I'd had it with feeling like a stepwife. I told her I thought we got married for the sake of Winston, in spite of the fact that I drove Teddy crazy, and he irked me to no end. Plus, I'd never forgiven him for the days when he was "out there." I told her that in counseling sessions with our therapist, Dr. Baham, I never felt we were making progress. I told her I thought Teddy had manipulated Dr. Baham to convince him that I was crazy.

"Did he say when he wants to see Winston?" she asked.

Strangely, I hadn't even thought about it up to that point, and Teddy hadn't mentioned how he wanted to handle visitation. For whatever reasons, I was feeling so possessive and afraid, I hoped he wouldn't bring it up.

"Why are you asking me that?" I asked.

"Well, I just thought you all might have worked that out," she said. "Your son will be better off if he sees his dad as much as he sees you."

A Good Friend

* A friend does not daddy bash (well, not often).
* A friend listens.
* A friend helps you plan for a peaceful future.
* A friend wants you to have psychological support.
* A friend does not play games with you and exploit your heartache.
* A friend helps you find the good in a bad situation.
* A friend steers you away from self-destructive behavior.

I let it slide, tried to ignore it, because I couldn't handle the thought of allowing Teddy what I considered to be one of the rewards of having a good marriage. I was mad at him, and I wanted him to suffer, even if the punishment included depriving my son of his own father. I was in deep denial at the time.

Darlene told me that she and her daughter's dad had fought like cats and dogs when Li'l Bit was a baby. It was hard on the girl, and she would often cry for no apparent reason. Those were sleepless nights, and Li'l Bit would wet on herself throughout the day. When Li'l Bit was with her dad for the weekend, she would only return to her mother after having temper tantrums. The daycare workers said she'd get angry easily and cling to toys. She didn't want to share.

Then, someone in their families set the two of them straight, letting them know there are rewards in being unselfish with the kids. Now Darlene was setting me straight.

Professional Help

I can't say that what Darlene had to tell me made much sense until a couple of months later. By then, I'd worked out a schedule where Teddy could see Winston every other weekend. But for whatever reasons, I still felt I was losing control, and that bothered me.

During a weekend visit to San Diego, Leon suggested I see a

counselor and possibly join a support group. When I went back home, I called my company's EAP coordinator and eventually ended up in a ten-week support group for single parents and their children. While the adults attended weekly two-hour sessions, our children met with child psychologists in a toy-filled room. Through role modeling, puppet shows, and stories, they learned how to deal with their feelings about being in single-parent homes. The first hour of the adult meeting was for parenting skills lessons. During the second hour, we focused on ourselves.

"Write down all the words people have used over the years to put you down. Each and every painful word. Write it down."

There were many tears, even sobs. Everyone wrote and wrote and wrote.

"Now, pick up your scissors and cut them out. Cut out each word."

We did as we were told.

"You're ugly."

"You have bad acne."

"You're stupid to think you'll ever be on TV again."

"You're just another statistic, a black single mother."

One by one, we read the insults. We ripped each one into shreds and placed them in a garbage can. After all, that's what they were—dirty words that deserved destruction. Finally, we were free, free to leave the garbage behind.

"Now, write down all the good things, all the encouraging things people have told you over the years."

We wrote slower this time. But eventually, our pages were full.

"Now cut them out."

Again, we followed instructions.

"Now, paste them on your posterboard."

We did. Then we went around to one another and got autographs, the way we did with our yearbooks in high school.

I posted my list in my room for at least a year, long enough for me to believe it without having to see it.

Meantime, Winston had drawn a happy face, a sad face, a scared face, and a "yipes" face, and we posted the faces on the refrigerator. That way, whenever his feelings manifested themselves in ways he couldn't explain, I'd have him point out a face and talk about it. And we talked a lot. Many times, I'd find myself pointing out his faces to describe my own feelings.

I learned a lot about parenting in the group. I learned the importance of getting your child to start talking to you when he or she is young so that it becomes a habit. I learned about "active listening," letting a person talk, but listening to and confirming how he or she is feeling. It really worked with Winston.

For example, one day, on our drive home from daycare, I asked him how his day went. He told me it was "bad," that no one wanted to play with him.

"You sound sad," I told him.

"I am sad, and I'm mad," he responded.

"So what do you think you'll do if no one wants to play with you tomorrow?"

"Be sad."

"Yeah, you could. But what else could you do?"

"Tell Mommy Estellee."

"Uh huh, you could. What else could you do?"

"Play by myself."

"Yeah."

"Or I could play with Eddie. He always plays by his self."

"You sure could."

Active listening is a good way to hear someone out without jumping to the rescue to solve a problem you weren't invited to solve. With children it encourages independence and responsibility. And it validates the kids' feelings.

In group, I learned this also works with adults. But it would take longer for that to sink into my thick head.

In the months to come, Teddy and I found peace—not love, mind you, but peace. The divorce was still not final. We'd procrastinated to a certain degree, and we hadn't worked out the details, but we were getting there.

Meantime, Teddy had already taken up dating. I had been checking out the brothers but hadn't made any real moves yet. But the thought of Teddy dating really unnerved me, especially after I found a pair of bloomers in the bag of dirty clothes Teddy sent back with Winston one Sunday night.

My heart pounded with furor. Not only was I angry that Teddy hadn't washed Winston's clothes (he never did), but he was actually careless enough to have allowed a pair of some woman's dirty drawers to be in the bag.

I dialed Teddy's number. There was no answer. Only the answering machine. What angered me further was the greeting he'd left on the machine: "You know what to do," Teddy's recorded voice said merrily.

"You know what to do?" I thought. I remember one time before I'd moved in with Teddy, he told me that when he got a machine, he'd put that greeting on it. Then later, during my pregnancy, after I learned Teddy had been sneaking around with some chick named Shana, I looked up her number in the New York City telephone directory and called it. When her machine came on, I heard her cutesy little recorded voice say, "You know what to do."

"Teddy, the next time you bring your son home, please have the decency to get your woman's (bleepity-bleep) drawers out of his dirty clothes bag. Not only are they dirty, they're *big!!*"

I slammed down the phone and calmed my hyperventilating behind down.

A couple of days later, my emotional stability was challenged yet again. It happened when I was giving Winston a bath.

"I like taking a bath with my toys," Winston said. "Do you and your daddy play with toys when he gives you a bath?" I asked.

"My daddy doesn't give me a bath. My other mommy does."

There was an awkward silence. My heart had fallen to the floor.

"What did you say?" I asked, hoping somehow I must have misunderstood.

"I said, my other mommy, Cynthia, gives me my bath when—"

"Winston, *don't you ever*—" I swallowed and took a deep breath. "Please don't ever call anyone but me your mommy. I am your only mother and I'll always be your only mother. Do you understand me?" Tears were leaking out of my bloodshot eyes.

"Yes, Mommy."

When You're Jealous of the "Other Mommy"

✳ Expect that you will feel jealous so it doesn't catch you too much off guard.

✳ Know that your children have the capacity to love other women, even those who have taken your place in their father's life.

✳ When your emotions get the best of you, take a time-out.

✳ Do not blame your children for your jealousy or anger.

✳ If you find you must say something to your children about your feelings, be honest. Admit you're jealous and tell your children it's going to take some time for you to get used to sharing them with someone else.

✳ Do not react emotionally in your child's presence; your child may begin to exploit your feelings, using them to manipulate you.

✳ Talk to girlfriends whom you trust.

✳ Write a list of positives and negatives about the situation, so that you can see in black and white that it's not as bad as it seems.

I let the water out of the tub and wrapped Winston in a towel and left the room as quickly as I could to gain my composure. I went to the refrigerator to get some cold water. I put my hand on the handle and came face to face with Winston's little drawings from his counseling session. I saw the happy face. I decided right away that I was feeling sad, angry, but mostly like the "yipes" guy. I was numb.

The next day, I talked to my friend, Ava, about it. Ava was in her late forties. She worked with me in public relations at AT&T and seemed to have an answer for everything.

Because I trusted Ava's advice, I listened carefully when she offered her support on my single-mamahood problem.

If You Need Counseling

* Ask a human resources manager at work whether you have an employee assistance program, and if so, check out counseling services available through it.

* Ask your family doctor about counseling services.

* Check with your pastor about support groups.

* Shop around, ask friends about counseling, and check in the Yellow Pages. Compare costs and always ask about sliding-scale payment plans.

* Check with your health plan (even if it's offered through your state) to see if it covers counseling.

* Call your local community centers to see if they offer cut-rate counseling services.

* Listen to people who love you; if they say you need help, they're probably right.

Note: A psychiatrist is a medical doctor, who can prescribe medications; a licensed clinical social worker or licensed marriage and family therapist may have a master's degree or a Ph.D and provide psychotherapy and counseling without medication.

"Girl, first of all, you need to quit trippin'," she said. "What did you expect him to do, be a monk?"

"No, Ava. But I didn't expect Winston to be calling some heifer his other mother."

"Girl, listen. It don't matter what he calls her. Winston knows you're his mother. You should be glad she's the kind of person he'd call his other mother. And you need to be glad somebody's helping Teddy's ass take care of your son. You know he don't know what the hell to do with no three-year-old."

I listened. This was something I hadn't considered.

"Just think of it as somebody taking good care of your son for free. Now Teddy has somebody else to do his work for him while he's in the streets. And you can be that much more comfortable to know your son's being taken care of. Shoot, girl, if I were you, I'd be partying real hard every other weekend. You should be thanking girlfriend for helping you out."

The next Monday, I went to group. I shared my story about the explosive incident with Teddy and Ava's advice. There were a couple of women in my group who were always complaining about how irresponsible their exes were to expose their children to "other women" so soon after their split-ups. One of them had been divorced for two years; another woman talked about how she was having a hard time dating, because every time her daughter saw her boyfriend, she'd have temper tantrums. The daughter was nine years old. As I thought about how silly I'd been, Alex and her son came into my mind. I felt so sorry for her and her family. They all had to suffer because she had not gotten over what happened with her ex. I realized she was making her son suffer by creating a problem for him. So what that he had two toothbrushes, I thought. Big deal! I vowed to try not to put that kind of trip on Winston, but that didn't mean this Cynthia woman didn't bother me.

5

Other Single Mamas

Single mamas need a support system. We need to know we're not alone. We need to listen to other women who have worn our shoes before. At the same time, we should share what we've learned, and yes, even the mistakes we've made with our sisters. Only then can we beat the odds and break the cycle.

Single mamas need one another. We can relate to one another's experiences. Darlene was more than a friend to me, she understood what I was going through in a way women who had not lived my experiences could not. Often the stigma of being a single mama keeps single mothers away from the women they need the most. But remember, single mamas who share close friendships are each other's most important resource.

We need each other for practical things, too. Try to team up with a single mama for babysitting and special outings. While you're hanging out, your kids can hang out. Your children will feel they're not alone.

Watch how your friends interact with their children. Learn from their successes and failures.

Children of single mamas often feel that they are the only kids who live without their fathers. When your kids see that other families function the way theirs does, they will begin to feel more whole.

Signs Your Child May Be Involved in a Gang

* Secretive behavior
* Hanging around with kids you don't know
* Dressing differently than usual
* Skipping school
* Behaving mysteriously, hard to locate, unwilling to account for whereabouts
* Wearing gang insignia (doodling, self-mutilation, graffiti)
* Taking drugs and alcohol

It is no accident that kids of single mamas have a tendency to gravitate toward groups. They crave family interaction and support. Too often, the groups in which your kids find themselves turn out to be "the wrong crowd" or, even worse, gangs. Single mamas' children want to feel they are okay, that they are accepted and acceptable. You can help them build this sense of empowerment when they are young.

When you first become a single mama, take your children to the library and find books about single-parent-headed households. Be honest. Tell them their family situation is not ideal, but let them know your family can be as loving as the best two-parent household. But don't try to persuade your children that they have it made because they're in a single-mama-headed household. If you try this false tactic, the kid will eventually realize it was nothing more than a con and you'll lose in the long run. Honesty is indeed the best policy.

Have married and single friends, but especially in the beginning, your single mama friends will be a great source of comfort. Only they can relate to what you're going through based on their own experiences. They can empathize and may be more willing to help when you need a shoulder to cry on or someone to keep your kids.

Winning Your Child Back

* Constantly say "I love you."
* Bombard your child with "family" messages, sharing family photos and other things that bond the family.
* Allow your child to share feelings without placing value on them. Just listen.
* Involve your child in structured activity (sports, music, church).
* Pair your child with an adult he/she admires for regular meetings.
* Let your child know you'll always be there.
* Love your child unconditionally.
* Provide consistent structure and discipline.
* Set curfews and make your child accountable for his or her whereabouts.
* Do not let your child scare you.
* Surprise your child with special treats that have always symbolized your special relationship (stop after school for ice cream, go for pizza, take in a movie together).
* Keep talking and keep listening.
* Find resources through your child's school, and use them!
* Remove your child from environment, from city to country for a while if possible.
* Encourage your child to work or volunteer in something he or she enjoys.
* Move to another city or across town if you have to.

(*Source:* Dr. Leon R. Kelley, pediatrician)

You'll begin to notice that you've always known single mamas, but until you became one yourself, you simply didn't pay much attention to them. Let single mamas you meet at school or church know your situation. Invite them over to your house so the kids can play. Offer to form a support group for single mamas at church. Before you know it, your children will come to you saying, "Hey, did you know Tony's parents are divorced?" Or, "Kim's mother's a single mom, too." The more your children deal with reality and stop hoping and praying that Mama and Daddy will one day find their way back to one another, the better. The reality of interacting with other single mamas and their kids may help.

If you don't have access to a network of single mamas, build one and head it yourself. Put a notice on your bulletin board at work or talk to your pastor about putting together a group from church. Plan monthly outings and distribute a telephone list. The network you establish will come in handy throughout your life.

If someone in your family has just become a single mama or is about to become one, give her a call and offer your support and advice. Do not allow her to form bad habits, to become an unhealthy single mama. There are too many single women out there raising their children without using the proper resources. Instead of preaching to these single mamas, simply share with them your own single-mamahood stories. Or give them a copy of this book. Eventually they'll get the hint. Their children and the world will be better because of it.

I am a strong believer in the institution of marriage, and I understand that a lot of time can pass before a couple decides that their bond needs to be broken. Sometimes the flame can be rekindled and these estranged relationships come back together. In the meantime, a mother in this kind of situation is a temporary single mama who needs support from other single mamas.

For whatever reasons, mothers whose husbands have died do not typically come to mind when we think of single mamas. But when these women go shopping or visit their children's schools, no one knows how or why the babies' father disappeared. These women are looked at as single mamas. They need the same support

---

Getting Past the Single-Mama Stigma

✳ Do not develop an inferiority complex.

✳ Be proud of your "single mama" status.

✳ Remind yourself that there are advantages to being a single mama (you're the boss, no one to answer to, fewer responsibilities, more choices, etc.).

✳ Don't try to read people's minds.

✳ Exchange stares with smiles.

✳ Always be the best you can be.

✳ Remind yourself that you're unique, special, and incredible.

---

other single mamas need, if not more. These women had no intention of becoming single mamas. Their marriages could have been perfect before their husbands died, and those husbands may have provided financially for the family. But a widowed single mama is still left to care for her children by herself. She is as much a single mama as you or I may be. She needs support from other single mamas more than she may know.

Sonya

I met Sonya while I was still at AT&T. I was a media relations manager, responsible for AT&T Universal Card Services, a new business headquartered in Jacksonville, Florida. My boss had asked me to put together a media prospectus for announcing the company's plans to open a remittance-processing center in Columbus, Georgia. I had conceived of a two-part press announcement. Part one would involve the Chamber of Commerce and other organizations we were working with to staff the new center; the second part would be held the day the center opened.

After the first news conference, a reporter and video photographer came up to me to chat and to learn a little about my job. They were pleasantly surprised to hear that I had been a TV news reporter at one time.

"You should meet our news director," the reporter told me. Then the photographer chimed in, "Doesn't she remind you of Sonya?" "Yeah, man, they have the same personality," said the reporter. "They're both hyper."

"Well, then, she must be a together woman," I said. "Is she black?"

"Yeah."

"And she's your news director?" I asked, surprised.

"Yeah," the reporter said. "I think she's one of only two or three black female news directors in the country."

They gave me Sonya's number, and I called her when I returned to my hotel room. We met a couple hours later in her office. After we watched the evening news, she invited me to her house for dinner.

Sonya's husband, David, was there when we arrived. He'd already started dinner. Their baby, D-Two, entertained David and me for a while until Sonya wrapped things up in the kitchen.

I grew closer to Sonya. About the time I finally got a full-time job at WTSP-TV in the Tampa/St. Petersburg, Florida, market, she'd gotten an assignment manager's job at WRAL-TV. That was the station I'd worked for in Raleigh for a few months during my pregnancy before I moved to New York to be with Teddy. We called each other a couple of times shortly after we started our new jobs, then several weeks went by, and I hadn't heard from Sonya. I sensed something was wrong. I called WRAL and was told that Sonya was on leave. There was an evasive note in the operator's voice, and when I pressed her for more information she told me that Sonya's husband had died.

I opened my mouth, but there were no words to fill the awkward silence. Finally, after a few seconds, I somehow mustered a good-bye, and just stared into space for a while from my desk.

David had died suddenly of a ruptured blood vessel. Sonya was called to the emergency room, and within a couple of hours, he was gone. Fortunately he left her with a couple of healthy insurance policies, but she also had two healthy babies by then, and no preparation whatsoever for single mamahood. But I must say, she's adjusting beautifully.

The thing that amazes me the most about Sonya is her ability to deal with her children's needs so calmly. She hardly ever raises her voice with the kids. When she does, she still sounds in control, not hysterical, as I sound when I lose it with Winston.

David is only about a year and a half older than his sister, Raven. He's quiet, but smart, like his daddy; Raven's talkative and inquisitive, and her brightness is apparent right away. Even when she was two years old, she'd hold complete conversations, using fully formal sentences.

Sonya and I talk on the phone an average of two or three days a week. In the time she has become a single mother, we have become best friends. Ironically she often thinks of me as her adviser, although much of my inspiration has come from her. I do remember a time not so long ago, however, when I was able to come to the rescue.

"Kelly, I need your help, girl."

"What's up?"

"These kids. I don't know what to do. I'm trying to get my Thanksgiving dinner ready, and they won't leave me alone."

"What are they doing now?"

"Well, D-Two's finally watching a video, but Raven's in the kitchen. She won't leave me alone. And she's getting in the way. She's following me around, and she's getting all whiny when I tell her 'Mommy's got to get the dinner done, and I can't do it with you on my tail.' I don't know if I'm being too mean. I'm yelling at her, and I don't know if that's fair."

"First of all, Sonya, stop beating yourself up. Of course you're being fair."

Single mamas need to understand that their children have to do their part. We sometimes think toddlers are too young to have to give up time and space, but this isn't true. Children begin to learn the importance of sharing with others as soon as you start teaching them. I told Sonya this was one of those teaching times.

"I think you're giving Raven mixed messages," I said. "She knows you're busy, but you're also reacting to her whining. She sees that it's working, and she's working on you. Tell her you're cooking and you can't do it with her in the kitchen with you. Give her two choices. Either she can go in the family room with D-Two and watch the video or she can go upstairs in her room to color."

"Yeah—and she'll say, 'Mommy, I want to color in here with you.'"

"No, Sonya. Tell her that was not one of the choices. Tell her if she can't make up her mind, she can go to bed. That's it. Be firm."

Sonya followed my advice, and Raven took her little tail upstairs. Within the hour, she had fallen asleep.

That night, Sonya prepared one of the most delicious Thanksgiving feasts imaginable—moist turkey, ham, collard greens, mixed vegetables, candied yams with pecans and marshmallows, fresh rolls, and to top it off, her famous red velvet cake. Sonya told me her mother was so impressed she accused her baby daughter of having the meal catered. Her guests weren't the only ones impressed— Sonya said little D-Two and even Miss Raven were proud as they could be. Raven told her mom she couldn't believe how pretty everything was. And having had a good night's sleep, she was an angel.

Guilt is something every good mother feels. It only becomes a problem when we let it get in the way of reason. Mothers, especially single ones, need to remember that parenting has a long-term goal. Our objective should be to bring up children who are self-assured, unselfish, and independent. The best way to do that is to set a good example.

Children can be extremely clever in their attempts to exploit our guilt. It becomes a power play. Sometimes Winston will ask me if my job at the TV station is more important to me than he is. On two occasions, he missed his bus home from school and called me an hour and a half from the time I was to go on the air with my health report to ask me to pick him up from school, which is thirty minutes away from my station. (I found someone to pick him up.)

Sonya told me Raven and D-Two start talking about their father when they want her attention. D-Two says he misses his dad. Raven, who barely remembers David, says she wants a new daddy.

Dealing with these matters of the heart and soul is difficult. Back

---

How to Avoid the Guilt Trip

✳ Bounce ideas off your single-mama friends.

✳ Listen to your children's feelings, but don't make their problem your problem.

✳ Let your child know in no uncertain terms that your time is your time.

✳ Make sure your children have their time with you, too.

---

in my support group, we concluded the best way to give kids attention is to give it when they least expect it. When our children are "yanking our chains," as Sonya puts it, we should ignore the attention attempts and stay focused on our needs. Later, while the episode is still fresh in our children's minds, we can talk to them about their feelings. We should let the kids know how hurtful it is to hear that we aren't giving enough. That usually puts a stop to the manipulation—for a while, anyway.

6

Dating

So what about your own needs? How do you handle your opportunities to meet a man so that you can have the chance of undoing your singlehood? This, I admit, is one of the most difficult aspects of being a single mama. Your situation doesn't prevent you from having opportunities to meet men and to date; it only means your opportunities will be limited. Your chances to meet men will often come with the exposures you'll have through your child. Instead of meeting men at nightclubs, happy hours, or fitness centers, you're more likely to meet them at school open houses and baseball games or track meets. You'll meet your children's friends' single or divorced fathers. You'll meet men at the mall or at the supermarket or at the park, usually when your child is with you. You can even use some of these occasions to see how your child responds to the man, and how he responds to your child.

Dating is a sticky issue. You really don't want your child to be exposed to every man you decide to check out. This takes creativity and cooperation, usually with another single mother. There's no need for your children to meet someone you're dating until your children and your prospective significant other are ready for it.

I've already mentioned a single mama's feeling that she must have a man in her life. When you meet a man, you have to deal with the "is this man going to be a good stepfather?" test on top of all your other questions about whether he's worthy. There will be times when you'll know in your heart you have no business with a certain man, but you'll have all kinds of pressure on you to have *someone* there, since for whatever warped reasons, society says any man is better than none.

"Where's Your Man?"

I have answered the questions, "Are you seeing anyone?" "Where's your man?" "Why doesn't a beautiful woman like you have someone special in her life?" too many times. And yet, almost in the same breath, I'm forced to defend myself against the self-righteous: "I hope you're not bringing all the guys you date to your house," "Your son does not need to be hurt by all your boyfriends," "Please don't let him get hurt or attached to your boyfriends," kind of remarks.

You're damned if you do, damned if you don't. So what's a single mama to do? I'm here to tell you, don't *listen* to all the people who are trying to run your life. You know in your heart what's right and what's wrong for your children. Your kids give you all the signals, whether you need them or not, to tell you when enough is enough with a certain man.

The dating game is probably a single mama's biggest challenge. For one thing, dating is very time consuming, and single mamas have little, if any spare time. If you worked the daddy thing out properly, you may have some holidays and long blocks of summer time to yourself. Those are really the best times to date. If you meet someone during the times that your children are with you, make sure he's worth it. Make him play by a special set of rules for single mamas.

The Dating "Game"

Always go into a new relationship expecting very little from the man. That way, you and your children will not be disappointed. Because of the pressures on single mamas to undo their single mamahood, they fantasize a lot about men they meet, expecting that every man they like will be "the one." It hurts me so much when I see a woman build up her expectations after one date with a guy, only to see her left hanging the next day when he doesn't call. Your best bet is to look at your time with a guy for what it is, a date— nothing more, nothing less.

You should always meet your date somewhere near your home, but not at your home until you get to know him pretty well. This takes at least eight or nine dates. The best time to go out is when your child is spending the night at friend's house.

Find out as much as possible about him, so that you can rule him out early if he's a loser. You should not be spending too much time at clubs and bars, but if you do happen to meet someone at one of those places, be extra careful. Single mamas have an undeserved reputation for being sluttish. If you must be a slut for a night, be careful. Do not—I repeat, do not—let this man know where you live. Your kids do not need to know about some man who only wants his mama for one thing, nor do young children need to know that their mama has those kinds of physical desires. That's between you, the man, and God.

The key to successful single-mama dating is putting everything in perspective. Remember, your primary objective in life right now is raising your children. This does not mean you can't have any fun, but it does mean you should look at dating for what it is—a chance to have male companionship, and a way to get to know several men so that you can recognize a good one when he comes along.

Above all, do not be desperate to change your single-mama status. Right now, you have the best of both worlds. You already have at least one child, so there's no rush to get married to have kids, and you also have your freedom. There's no one bugging you about how you clean your house or cook your dinner or discipline your kids. There's no one checking his watch when you walk in the door or pouting because you don't spend enough time with him.

In other words, with intelligence and care, you have another chance to pick a man who really deserves you. You're a whole person with a lot of responsibilities; you don't need another major responsibility right now. If a man cannot be a true partner to you, someone who gives as much as he takes, someone who truly adds to the quality of your life, you don't need him. Single mamahood isn't that bad.

As a single mama, you get to have a man when you want and tell him to leave when you're tired of him. You know how to make a living, you have your own debts, and you run your own show. Always keep that in mind when you're considering whether a man is worth having in the life you share with your children.

Dealing With Superman

Often men will come into the picture trying to "rescue" you. They're so used to hearing about how single mamas want a man and need a man, that they honestly think they're doing you a favor just by showing up. You need to let men know up front that you can take them or leave them and you can "do bad" all by yourself. These supermen who want to rescue you believe your kids need a daddy. You need to set them straight on this, too. Let them know that your kids already have a daddy. Although having the right stepfather in the home would be nice, Superman should not expect to walk into your life and take over, "fixing" your "broken" home.

I've talked to too many kids who resent their formerly single mamma and their new stepdad. They hate how Mama was so weak and so needy, she turned her whole life and freedom over to some control-freak man. They miss their life with their single mama who seemed to have more money and to be happier when she was alone.

Appreciating Freedom

Single mamahood is an institution that has its advantages. One of them is being free to raise your children the way you want, without a man who barely knows them trying to take over. I know I sound like a male-basher, but I'm not. It's just that I see too many single mamas buying the hype about two-parent homes. An ideal two-parent home is a home where a child's biological parents raise their children. The next best thing is either a stepparent-two-parent home where the stepparent observes until he's figured out how to fit in, or a single-mama household where the single mama has her head on straight.

Keep your head on straight. Take your time. Your kids are worth it.

Andrew

By the time we'd moved to Florida, I had dated several men on those every-other weekends that Teddy had Winston. But none of the guys was special. Until Andrew, I hadn't wanted to introduce any of them to Winston as my boyfriend.

I met Andrew a couple months before I was to move to Florida to take the new position with AT&T. I had attended the Magic Johnson celebrity dinner to benefit the United Negro College fund; a star-studded event attended by L.A.'s finest. Many a male friend of mine might have mistaken it for heaven. All the beautiful people and the not-so-beautiful were there looking their best.

I was outside waiting for the valet to bring my car when I caught Andrew's eye. He was leaning on a crutch, which I learned was the result of a knee operation from a skiing accident. I wish for the life of me that I could remember the conversation, but all I can recall is having said something very aggressive to him. We struck up a conversation and ended up exchanging numbers.

Andrew has got to be the nicest man I've ever dated—no conceit, no airs, just plain old nice. Our conversations lasted for hours. He told me many times that our first date was the best date he ever had.

Winston was with Teddy during our courtship. It was the end of the summer, and at the time, Teddy and I knew we'd both be moving out of state soon, so he was keeping Winston pretty much the whole summer.

When we returned from our first date, Andrew and I spent hours talking about our families, lives, and dreams. He was so sweet,— and actually nervous. We held hands. Then we engaged in the most tender kiss I'd ever experienced. It was so passionate, so romantic, that I had to send Andrew home. It was too much for me to handle.

After that first date, we saw each other constantly, and things were great. I invited Andrew to my brother's wedding, which was to take place in Los Angeles in a few weeks.

I was so proud of Andrew. I loved being with him, loved talking to him, loved talking about him. He made me feel pretty again, and special. He'd do anything for me. I knew I was capable of falling in love again.

Finally, it was the weekend of my brother Jimmy's wedding to his fianceé, Marinna. The movers had arrived at my house the day before, and the clothes I'd take with me to Florida were at Andrew's. Winston was to be the ring bearer and I'd picked up his tuxedo and shoes earlier. We were ready to go.

"Mommy," Winston whined. "My shoes are too big."

"Winston, don't worry about it. You'll be okay." He cried. "How can I walk down the aisle? How can I be uncle Jimmy's ring bear?"

We were already late. We got in Andrew's car, with Winston in the backseat, and he started crying again. "I can't be the ring bear."

"Winston, I'll tie the shoes, it'll be okay."

I thought about how cute Winston was, calling himself the ring "bear." But the cuteness didn't last long. Winston bean to wail. "Just shut up," Andrew said, looking in the rear-view mirror.

"What did you say?" I asked Andrew.

"I'm sorry."

"Oh, no," I said in a low monotone. "You told my son to shut up. *That* is unacceptable."

During the entire wedding, even at the reception through champagne, wine, and whatever else I drank that night to calm my nerves, that's all I could remember—*shut up*. . . . I believe I forgave Andrew, but I never forgot.

Two months later, Winston and I had moved into our new house in Jacksonville. He had enrolled in his new preschool, I was in the groove on my new job, and Andrew was coming to Florida to pay us a visit. In the interim, there had been numerous long-distance phone calls, flowers, and I love yous. I had dismissed the "shut up" as a fluke. When we picked Andrew up at the airport, Winston seemed happy to see him, and Andrew seemed happy to see both of us.

I think the first day went okay. But the second day was D-Day. We walked into the house, and Winston dropped his backpack on the floor, against the wall, just inside the front door. It's where he had always deposited it when we came into the house.

"Winston, pick that up," Andrew demanded.

"I don't have to," Winston replied.

Winston didn't mean any disrespect. It was his way of saying that his mother doesn't make him put the backpack in his room or anywhere in particular. I'm sure he wondered why this guest in our home would suddenly be concerned about where we put things in our house. I wondered, too.

Then there was the incident involving a favorite toy of Winston's. He was upstairs playing with his prized Teenage Mutant Ninja Turtle toy when he began to cry.

"Andrew!" he yelled. "Can you come help me fix my Teenage Mutant Ninja Turtle elevator?"

There was silence.

"Andrew!" Winston begged. "Please come help me fix my Teenage Mutant Ninja Turtle elevator!"

Again, silence.

"Andrew?" I asked. By the time I could get the next words out, Winston was downstairs. His face was wet with tears.

"Andrew," he repeated. "Please come fix my Teenage Mutant Ninja Turtle sewer elevator."

"How'd it break?" Andrew asked in a couldn't care-less manner.

"Donatello broke it," Winston answered.

"How'd it break?" Andrew repeated, as if Winston hadn't answered the first time.

Meantime, I was sitting there wanting to butt in, but figuring Winston could handle this one. Even at age four, he knew Andrew was trying to get him to say he'd broken the toy. But to Winston, even though he was playing with the toy, it was Donatello the Turtle who was attempting to take a ride in the elevator when it broke. And besides, it wasn't that important. The result was the toy was broken, and Winston wanted to give Andrew a chance to redeem himself with him and his mother by fixing it. The only problem was, Andrew didn't get it. He was competing with Winston—going head to head with a four-year-old, stubbornly refusing to see that Winston was extending a peace offering and a bonding opportunity. And I admit it, he also was trying to get Andrew out of my space for a moment. But more important, Andrew wasn't willing to pay a small price for what could be a pleasant trip to Florida and an opportunity to grow in his relationship with Winston and myself.

"Donatello broke it," Winston repeated.

You Like Him, He Likes You, Your Child Hates Him (or Vice-Versa)

✳ Realize your family life is doomed if your children and significant other can't get along.

✳ If the significant other is worth keeping, force him and your children to spend time together without you.

✳ Be honest with your significant other about your feelings toward him and your children.

✳ Realize you're only further complicating your life by allowing a man your children don't like or respect into your life.

✳ If it's worth it, give it time; time has a way of healing and breaking tension; maybe they'll grow on one another.

"You broke it," Andrew demanded.

"Uh-uh," Winston whined. "Donatello was going up the elevator, and it just broke."

"You broke it," Andrew repeated.

I wish I could remember how the conversation ended. I believe I finally got into it and explained to Winston that Andrew believed it was he who'd broken the elevator and not Donatello, because he was the one who'd placed Donatello on the elevator. Either Andrew or I finally went upstairs to fix the elevator. Then I explained to Andrew that Winston was not being dishonest with him, but Andrew just didn't get it. Needless to say, Andrew got fired. During his trip—a trip he ended up cutting short—he slept on the couch in that very den where the awkward exchange between himself and my child had taken place.

Michael

I met Michael at an event called First Friday. There are First Friday chapters across the country, and they provide an opportunity for

African-American professionals to mix and mingle. On this particular First Friday, I was helping a friend put together a dating game.

"Will you be one of our bachelors?" I asked a rather built, well-dressed young man.

"I already am," he answered. "Are you one of the bachelorettes?"

"No," I answered. "I'm the game show host." My name's Kelly Williams."

"I'm Mike Flowers," he responded. "I've met you before. I gave you a card for my karate dojo, and you told me you'd call because you wanted your son to take karate."

By then, Winston was five years old. Because I'm kind of spacey sometimes, I only vaguely remembered meeting Michael before. But I knew I had one of his business cards.

The next time I saw Michael was at the downtown Jacksonville Boys and Girls Club. Winston had arrived for his first karate lesson; he was very excited. I'd already instructed myself not to push Winston into this on account of my interest in the karate teacher, but I knew that first class would be an opportunity for me to see this hunk of man again.

I dropped Winston off and returned to pick him up about an hour later. Michael told me he thought Winston would be a big success at karate. When we got home that night, I felt a quiet calm. There was something special about Michael, and I thought he might be "the one."

About a week after Winston's first karate class, the two of us were at home on a Friday night with nothing to do.

"Mommy, can I have a party for Snooky?" he asked. Snooky was Winston's stuffed bear. "It's his birthday today."

"Sure. Who do you want to invite?"

"Charles and Chris, Miss Barbara [his babysitter], Big Ant' [her husband], Anthony [their child], and Michael."

"Okay, can I invite some people, too?" I asked.

"Yeah."

I told Winston we could have the party the next day. I got on the phone that night and called everyone to tell them that as silly as it sounded, they were invited to a birthday party for Winston's teddy bear.

The beginning of the party was for Snooky and the kids. They ate hot dogs, played pin the tail on the donkey and musical chairs. We had a cake for Snooky and the kids even sang "Happy Birthday." It was a decent little last-minute party.

Later the kids went upstairs to Winston's room, and the party really got moving downstairs. We played cards, danced, ate, drank, and had a fun time. It was a good chance for me to check out Michael in another setting, and I liked what I saw. He was gentle and quiet, not real outgoing at all, but gracious. My only disappointment was that he was one of the first to leave.

But the next afternoon, he called to invite me to the movies that next Friday night. Winston stayed with friends the night of my big date, and everything went as planned. Michael showed up on time looking fine.

We chatted and laughed a lot on the way to the theater. Unfortunately, *Prince of Tides* was a lot more popular than we'd anticipated, so there was a long wait for the tickets.

After the movie, we went for a drink at a little jazz club. When Michael took me home, he gave me a hug and told me he had a great time. The next day, he came over for dinner. Winston was home and played with him for a little while, while I cooked. When I walked into the family room, I smiled to myself. Winston had just jumped on Michael's lap. "Mommy, he feels like my dad," he said.

Of course, that made me like Michael even more. Like many single mamas, I'd fantasized about what it would be like to have a great stepfather for my son. And after the Andrew experience, I told myself the relationship between the man of my dreams and my son had better be strong, or it wouldn't work.

I'm not sure whose fault it was, but the mistake I made with Michael was that I let his relationship with my son develop much faster than his relationship with me.

I think a lot of it had to do with the fact that Michael had a very strong Christian background, and, unlike other men I knew, he didn't approach our relationship with a sexual goal in mind. He also wasn't into gossiping and was uncomfortable talking about anything too touchy-feely. A lot of that came from his military training. Michael was a Naval Academy graduate who was working as a

Jacksonville Electric Authority manager. (He did the karate thing in the evenings.)

A month after we met, Michael and I seemed to run out of things to say to one another. I have a tendency to push people to open up and talk about their feelings before they're really ready. At the same time, I love feeling close to people, and one of the best ways to build a bond of intimacy is to get beyond discussing things to talking about feelings. But Michael was not down with that—not at all.

However, my relationship with Michael was the catalyst for the biggest change I've made in my life. He went to church regularly, more than anyone I'd ever known. He was there Sunday mornings and nights as well as Wednesday nights. He also was involved in a very active Christian singles group. I found myself going to all the services Michael went to, in addition to a Monday night Bible study with the singles group. Even though I was raised Catholic before my mother's divorce from my father and her remarriage to Leon, I knew very little about religion. I didn't know that adults can be baptized when they choose to accept that Jesus Christ's death was the price paid for our sins so that we could still have life after death. When I learned this, it didn't take me long to make the choice myself. I studied the Bible a lot, and it was the most enjoyable learning experience I have ever had.

Meantime, I'd quit my job as media relations manager at AT&T Universal Card Services and had begun to teach full time as a visiting associate professor in the Communications and Visual Arts Department at the University of North Florida. At the same time, I was freelancing as a reporter for WJXT-TV, so I was working sometimes seven days a week.

Because it was so important to Michael to have Winston practice karate, he would often pick him up for me and keep him when I was working. Needless to say, Michael spent far more time with Winston than he did with me.

The next December, while Winston was in New York with his father, I was offered and accepted a full-time reporting job at WTSP-TV in Tampa–St. Petersburg. By the time Winston returned from that Christmas holiday, we were living in a new city and he was at a new school. Then one day, about three weeks after I started the new

---

Helping Your Kids When Ending a Relationship

* Explain what's happening.
* Encourage your children to have and express their own feelings about your ex.
* Allow kids to accept occasional outings with your ex, but space them so that your ex cannot "use" your children to manipulate you. Phase out these outings eventually.
* Allow kids to keep gifts and continue to display photos, etc.
* Expect that sometimes the breakup will be as hard on children as it is on you.
* Do not try to replace your ex with a rebound substitute.
* Involve a counselor, if necessary.

---

job, Michael called me to say that whatever we had was over—that he and I had too many differences.

Lots of people, men and women, have cautioned me not to let my son get close to too many men, but I understand how easy it is to make that mistake. And when you're a single African-American professional woman who happens to favor single African-American professional men, it's hard to find that one right man and stick to him. After a short period of time, you're usually ready to end the relationship and quite frankly, you know your kid is going to help you decide whether the guy you're interested in is a suitable mate. So this is a mistake I believe I've made, but fortunately, I haven't seen any negative side effects. Maybe what people are saying is that you don't want your children to be exposed to sexual flirting and playing between yourself and men you're not married to. Since I've been able to avoid that mistake, maybe that's why my son doesn't seem to be bothered by the number of men I've dated. Besides, he loves his father, and despite the fantasies I might have had, he never shared with me any dreams of any man I've dated taking Teddy's place.

7

Steps

Eventually your children's father is likely to find himself another woman, and at some time or another, he'll probably make her his wife. This opens up a whole new set of issues for a single mama to deal with.

Many single mamas look at the stepmother as an adversary, or at least a rival. They do everything they can to discourage a positive relationship between their children and the kids' stepmother. This is unhealthy because it can teach your kids how to hate. It can also make visits to their father stressful and unpleasant. I'm not saying you have to be buddy-buddy with the wife of your children's father, but you should be civil. Eventually you and the stepmother may even grow to be friends. Just remember, the closer the relationship between your kids' stepmom and yourself, the better for your children.

There will be many times you'll call to talk to your children's father and the stepmother will answer the telephone. You should be cordial and always ask her how she's doing. If she wants to have an attitude, let her. Her bitterness is her problem. Just be nice and accomplish what you set out to do.

If you do have animosity toward the stepmother, try not to share your feelings in your children's presence. If you think she's being unfair to your kids in any way, gather all your facts and present them to their father. Let him deal with her. You stay out of it.

Sometimes members of your family will interfere with how you deal with the stepmother issue. People are simply not used to the "can't we all just get along?" attitude. They'll instigate problems by asking questions about your ex's and his new wife's home and car. "What kind of ring did he buy her?" "He didn't do all that for you." These are things you don't need to hear. You have to remind yourself that this woman is stuck with your ex and all his problems, but she is also someone who will be involved in the lives of your children for some time, perhaps forever. So it's best to bury the hatchet and move on.

Moving On

You might need to sit down and make a list of all the stepmother's good points when it comes to how she treats your children. If she's smart, don't be afraid to admit it. If she has good taste in clothes or knows how to braid your girls' hair better than you can, admit that, too. This way, you can always pull out the list when things get edgy, which, at some point, they will.

Once you're mature enough, and if you think she can handle it, contact your children's stepmother to let her know your feelings. If you're somewhat jealous, admit it, but tell her you realize she has many strengths that will be beneficial to your kids. Chances are she will not trust you right away. In time, though, that icebreaker will pave the way for easing tension when the two of you need to talk about the kids.

If you're doing all the other things right about making sure your kids spend enough time with their father, they'll also spend a lot of time with their stepmother. Incidents will arise where she will need to discipline them. If you leave the communications lines open, the two of you can work together.

Enough Love to Go Around

Again, realize that love is not a pie that can be cut only into so many finite pieces. The more people your children learn to love,

---

Steps to Dealing With Steps

* Do not hold your ex's choice of someone else against her.
* Help the stepmother to be a good parent to your children by sharing with her your parenting philosophy.
* Communicate as frequently as possible.
* Allow children to love their stepmother.
* Make the stepmother the point of contact for invitations to any special events (birthday parties, graduations, recitals, etc.).
* Always respect the stepmother's home and time.
* Do not allow your friends and family to trash the stepmother or her family.

---

the more balanced they'll be emotionally—the better their behavior, and the better their performance in school.

Your children may end up with stepbrothers and stepsisters, or later, with half-siblings. I don't care how you feel about these kids, your children have the right to love them. Do not look for the bad in these kids; look for the good, because nine times out of ten, they'll end up spending a lot of time with your children, sometimes in your home.

You cannot ignore these kids when your children have birthday parties and other get-togethers with their friends. Often your children will ask you if their stepbrothers or half-sisters can stay overnight. Unless you know for a fact that these kids are a bad influence on your kids, that they're giving them marijuana or encouraging them in other harmful ways, do not discourage these relationships. I've heard some single mamas get all crazy when their kids call one of their step siblings "brother" or "sister" without the prefix, "step." That's your kid's business, not yours, so stay out of it.

Anytime you're feeling threatend by one of your children's stepfamily members, you're the one with the problem. You need to check yourself and explore your true feelings until you can come up with an honest explanation for what's going on. Then deal with the real feeling, not with stuff that doesn't matter. Remember, you are trying to nurture what is positive and good in your children. You don't want them to be petty and trifling, and you musn't be that way, either.

Cynthia

While I was trying to make the transition back into television, I seized every networking opportunity that came my way. When I heard about a conference sponsored by the National Association of Environmental Journalists to be held in Ann Arbor, I signed up.

The Ann Arbor trip turned out to be just what I had planned. It was an opportunity for Winston to visit his dad while I did my thing at the conference. But in another way, that trip became one of the most pivotal events in my relationship with Cynthia, Winston's stepmother.

Teddy picked Winston and me up from the airport in Detroit—he offered. It was actually one of his first acts toward a peace offering. The trip was pleasant, but peculiar. It was weird because Teddy told me Cynthia wanted me to come over for dinner the next day. At that point, I had never spent any time with my son's stepmother—this would be a first. I wasn't sure I was ready, but I said, sure.

Teddy and Cynthia had gotten married about the time I quit my AT&T job. Shortly after that, I learned they were expecting a child. I wondered why Teddy would jump from the skillet into the fire, but, hey, it was none of my business.

Since my mother's divorce from my father, the two of them have never spent any time together, except, of course, in court. I had no model for how this should be done. My mother always gave me the impression that the best way to deal with an ex is not at all. You should go along, minding your own business, and definitely never letting him know any of your weaknesses and shortcomings. Let his imagination go wild so he can regret all the mistakes he made with you, but I'm far too touchy-feely for that approach.

Dinner was fine and Cynthia was gracious. Winston gave me a tour of the house. To my surprise, I was not jealous at all; I was actually happy for Teddy. It seemed that he and Cynthia were compatible. Their home was decorated the way Teddy likes things—very cozy and very New England.

Here are just some of the questions I've been confronted with from members of my family since my divorce: "Why would you go to *his* house for dinner?" "You shouldn't let him know what's going on in your life." "Do you really think that woman likes you, or was she just letting you in her house to please her husband?" "What was Teddy trying to do?" "Was he trying to make you jealous or hurt you?"

I've learned that other single mothers who wish to continue a relationship with their children's father for the sake of the kids hear similar questions.

Your parents and family are often so bitter and angry at your ex for allowing the family to break up and their own fairy tale to have an unhappy ending, that they want to end it all. They never want to see him again.

Many parents and siblings of single women secretly, and sometimes even openly, hope a new daddy will come along and make everything okay. In their hearts, they think it would be best and simpler for everyone if that mean old ex-husband or ex-boyfriend who biologically fathered your children were dead. At least he should play dead.

This is where you have to step in and lovingly show that there is a better way. By example, your family will learn to break the cycle of denial and anger. Then, they, too, will be free to share their love for the father.

My parents have come to accept that Teddy is a big part of Winston's life; they call his house during summers when Winston's there. They even make arrangements with Cynthia and Teddy for Winston to spend some time with them during the summers.

My relationship with Cynthia has grown in ways I would have never expected. The winter before my trip to Ann Arbor, Teddy and Cynthia were spending Christmas in Los Angeles. They hadn't gotten married yet, and my family hadn't quite accepted the idea of Teddy being with anyone other than me.

It was my turn to have Winston for Christmas, but since I had to work many of the days that Winston would be off, I asked my parents if I could send him to be with them in San Diego. Of course, they agreed. Since Teddy and I communicate regularly, he was aware that he and Winston would be in California at the same time. I assumed he'd call my parents and arrange a time to pick up Winston to take him to L.A. for a few days.

On Christmas day, I called my parents' house to wish Winston and everyone else a Merry Christmas. I spoke to my parents first, then my brothers and sisters. Everyone, starting with my parents, told me in hushed tones that Teddy and Cynthia were there. They all thought it was odd, if not awkward to have Teddy and his new girlfriend in the house on such a special day, while I was thousands of miles away. To me, it was more amusing than anything else. In fact, the funniest part was that my family was far more uncomfortable with what was going on than I was.

Of course, after dealing with the siblings, I spoke to Winston. He was in his world. He was so happy that his dad was there to help him enjoy his holiday. To him, there was nothing unusual at all about the fact that his dad and Cynthia were at his grandma's house. He was just happy to be with people he loved.

About a year after Teddy and Cynthia married, Cynthia gave birth to an incredibly beautiful little girl named Zora. Winston finally had the sibling he had always wanted (actually, he would have preferred a boy), and I didn't even have to be fat for nine months and go into labor for it to happen. He was ecstatic the first time he saw Zora, and called me from Ann Arbor to describe her in detail.

"Mommy, you should see my sister," he said. "She has red hair, real curly red hair, and she's real big. She has fat cheeks; she's so cute."

It was a wonderful moment. I shared in my son's happiness. When I hung up the phone, I stared into space and smiled. I couldn't believe that I'd come so far, that the woman I once felt so threatened by had brought my son and myself so much happiness.

I give Winston a birthday party every other year, and on his eighth birthday, the theme was dinosaurs. The kids had a dinosaur egg hunt. I put little dinosaur toys in plastic Easter eggs, and some of the eggs contained money. I also bought little rubber eggs that you're supposed to put into hot water. After a minute or so, they actually hatch to reveal baby dinosaurs. The kids loved it. The cake was decorated with dinosaurs, and the pinãta was in the shape of Barney—the one dinosaur eight-year-old boys love to hate.

Teddy had called me several weeks before the party to tell me that he, Cynthia, and Zora were going to be in Florida around the time of Winston's birthday and they planned to go to Disneyworld. He wanted to make arrangements to pick Winston up to join them.

I told him I thought it would be a great idea if they could surprise him at his birthday party. He and Cynthia agreed it would be a wonderful surprise.

During the party, I'd started to worry. We'd gotten through the introductions, dinosaur egg hunt, egg hatching, pin the tail on the donkey, musical chairs, and just about everything but the cake and gifts, and there was no sign of Winston's dad and stepmom.

I'd stalled for a while, but I knew some of the parents were going to be on time to pick up their children, so the show had to go on. The kids and some of their parents who'd stayed for the party had just finished singing "Happy Birthday." Winston closed his eyes to make a wish, and by the time his eyes opened, Teddy, Cynthia, and Zora were in my kitchen. Winston opened his eyes and just stared at them for a few seconds. His eyes welled up with water and he dashed over to his other family to give them big hugs and kisses. He was so proud of his sister, "Look, everybody," he told them. "This is my sister, Zora. I told you she has fat cheeks. And this is my dad and my stepmom." The crybaby I am, I just let the tears flow. I gave Teddy and Cynthia my own hugs. I was so proud of them, and so proud of myself. I knew we had something special, something that made me feel good about myself, made me feel strong and loving.

I have grown to love Cynthia. She's a good stepmom to my baby, and she hung in there with Teddy long enough to give Winston a beautiful little sister.

In recent years Teddy and Cynthia have had marital difficulties. She talks to me because she knows I'm the one person who can

---

When Your Friends and Family Don't Get It

* Give them time, it takes a while to get used to civil step families; people just aren't used to it.

* Trust doesn't come overnight; it took you a while; it'll take them longer.

* Stick to your guns; let your family know that you know it's in your best interest to make the relationship work.

* Invite everyone to the kids' special functions; anyone who has a problem can stay home.

* If all else fails, share this book with your family.

---

understand how she could consider "letting such a good man go." Cynthia and I have been confiding in one another since a few months before their wedding. It started with a heart-to-heart that I initiated to let her know that there were no hard feelings on my part toward her. I wanted her to know that I've always appreciated how well she takes care of my son, and that I knew she must be a special woman because of that. I wanted to wish her well in her marriage to Teddy. I told her it would be excellent for my son to have such a great stepmother.

When I first told my mother about my relationship with Cynthia, she warned me to be careful. She wasn't used to these kinds of relationships working. Cynthia told me all of her friends and her mom thought it was a little strange at first, too. But for us, it works. It works when Winston is in New York and Cynthia has a problem with him. It makes me comfortable about what's going on in my son's life when I can't be with him. Above all else, it keeps the peace, and it makes Winston happy.

I hope that Winston won't have to witness the breakup of his daddy and stepmother. It would be hard for him. I know he doesn't remember my divorce from Teddy; he was too young. But he's certainly felt the effects. I don't want him to have to experience all of this again. He loves both Teddy and Cynthia, and he thinks the world of his little sister. Once again, his life would be in turmoil over his parents' inability to make things work.

Cynthia and I talked about what we could do to make the separation easier on Zora and Winston. If necessary, we'd visit one another whenever possible, and to try to take vacations together with the kids. That way, Winston wouldn't lose his "other mommy" or his little sister.

Cynthia would become a single mama, and I'm doing everything I can to help.

For now, Cynthia's working and I am praying, hoping it won't come to that.

8

Work

Work is a whole other ballgame when the employee is a single mama. Just being a mother puts you in a challenging position, but when you're a single mama, sometimes you have to work three times as hard just to get the job done.

When your children discover stay-at-home moms, you'll have yet another problem on your hands. Your kids will actually compare you to these women and try to make you feel guilty for having a job. "Why can't you be like so-and-so's Mom?" you'll hear.

We live in a country that has not yet made up its mind about single mamas and work. We feel that it's wrong for women to collect welfare and keep having babies. Yet, at the same time, we crucify any woman who leaves her children alone or in the hands of inadequate daycare providers in order to go to work. It's a real Catch 22. But suffice it to say, if you're a single mama, you have to provide for your children, so you have to go to work.

Convenience

If at all possible, find a job close to home and close to where your children attend school. Also, find a support network—someone in your family or someone in your neighborhood ready to "have your back" if something should come up with one of your kids while you're at work. You have to have a "what if" plan to put into play should one of your kids get sick at school, miss the bus, or get locked out of the house. You will not be able to leave work for every possible contingency, or you'll eventually be an at-home mom with no income. Talk to your kids about this so they'll know what to expect and understand what's going on.

Employers and coworkers often assume single mamas will not be good employees, because they know that if you're a good mama, you'll put your children first. You must understand, though, that putting your children first does not mean you'll always be the person who comes to their rescue.

Your support network also will have to help you out if travel is involved in your job. Make sure you never bemoan the issue of how hard it is juggling your kids and your job responsibilities to your boss or coworkers. Whenever someone tries to get me to reveal my concerns in this area, I just say it's something African-American women have been doing since slavery, which is the truth. Just take care of it quietly. You'll often hear married moms and dads bring up family matters when they're asked to do something at work that might interfere with what's going on at home; that does not give you license to do the same. The advantage married parents have over single mamas is that they're entitled by society's rules to care out loud about their children. If your boss asks you to do something that interferes with your parenting, simply say, "No problem," and get on the telephone with your support folks as soon as possible.

No Such Thing as a Free Lunch

At the same time, you must also take care of your support folks. Give them free tickets that you might get for concerts, send them flowers every now and then, or take them a plate when you have time to cook dinner. Pick up their favorite delicacy from the grocery store. Constantly let them know how much you appreciate them. This will help you immensely when you need them; it also will keep you from feeling too guilty when you need these people. Also, try not to use your support network when you just need to hang out with the girls after work or when you want to hook up with some man. That's like crying wolf. When you really need the support, it may not be there.

At work, you must work harder than the rest of the folks. Don't use up a lot of your on-the-job time gossiping with coworkers. Instead, smile and remind them that this is just one of your jobs, so you have to get your business taken care of within the allotted eight hours. If they don't understand, they're not worth your time; they clearly are not interested in helping you to be successful on the job.

Believe it or not, many people will admire you to the point of envy. They'll know through your example that a single mama can do it all. It will remind them of their shortcomings, because even though you have two jobs, you'll be outperforming them. That's their problem, girlfriend. Just keep on keeping on.

Childcare Resources

Child Care Centers   Usually affordable, fees may be based on a sliding scale. Often fees are adjusted for more than one child. Usually structured and regulated by city and/or state. Kids learn to interact with others. Disadvantages include little personal attention. You may be charged exorbitant late charges if you are not at the center on time to pick up your child. Also, if your child is sick, has chicken pox, sometimes even a runny nose, she may not be permitted to attend. Transportation may be provided for older children who need to be picked up from school.

Family Daycare   My favorite. Typically, city business affairs departments or welfare offices keep lists of providers in your area. These are families that care for a limited number of children in their homes. Fees are set down based on a sliding scale, but usually are adjusted for more than one child. Your children may get more personalized care. Often family care providers are flexible with single mamas who may not be able to make it on time to pick up their children. Sometimes they'll provide reasonable after-hour care or off-hour babysitting at reasonable rates. Family care providers may have "sick" rules, but are often more flexible than other daycare providers if your kids are sick.

Nanny This is where the sitter is in your home. It can be very expensive. I've never been able to afford a nanny, even on a middle-class salary. Advantages include having someone at your house full-time to cook, clean, and tend to your children's every need. Sometimes the nanny can even provide transportation to and from your child's activities.

At-School Care This may be provided by your school in the early mornings and afternoons. There are many advantages. You can make it to work on time, knowing your children are already at school. It's typically very affordable, based on a sliding scale, according to what you can afford. Kids usually enjoy it, since it gives them time to be with their friends. After school, there may be tutors to help your children with their homework.

Recreation and Neighborhood Center Care This is typically provided before and after school. It's usually not as structured as daycare. It's ideal for older children who have self-discipline. The children are usually required to do their homework after school, then other activities are provided. If your children are easily swayed by peer pressure, this is not necessarily for them. Although there is adult supervision, there are many distractions; kids can easily slip away and get into trouble. However, if your children are involved in sports, this is ideal. Typically recreation centers provide every sport your children would be interested in. It's a way to give you a little more time at the office, since sports time usually extends after the after-school care is over. Again, irresponsible or immature children don't do well with the kind of freedom offered by these programs.

The Boss

My schedule was crazy when I became a general assignment reporter at a Tampa–St. Petersburg TV station. The hours I worked depended on what stories broke each day. One of the first things I did when I moved to St. Petersburg was to run an ad in the newspaper for a babysitter. I found someone I liked a lot. She was a daycare worker at a major corporate daycare center who wanted to make some extra money for her upcoming wedding. After running a complete police and reference check on her, I felt safe enough to have her pick Winston up from his school's after-care program and keep him at my place until I arrived home.

Sometimes I'd also need her to be "on-call" for me. The biggest drag was that even in the beginning, even before I'd been on my job a week, I realized my boss was sadistic. It seemed the more she admired me, the more she'd try to mess with my head. She knew Winston was my weak spot.

I had been on the job four days. On Friday, she informed me that I'd be on call the weekend. Fortunately I'd already worked out the babysitter thing, so it wasn't a problem. Also, I'd already learned not to give any employer the benefit of the doubt when it comes to understanding the challenges of a single mama.

That Sunday night, when I was called in to cover a fire, I picked up the phone to call my babysitter, who lived in the apartments across the street. By the time I was dressed, she was there. I know my boss expected me to say I couldn't be on call, let alone carry out the assignment, because of my son. Actually, the fire didn't even require a reporter. It could have easily been shot by a photographer and handled in a "read" by one of the anchors. That's how we usually handle fires, unless we have knowledge that people were involved. In this case, the burned building was an abandoned church. I did make an interesting story out of it, since I found someone who'd attended church there in the old days. But I was being tested. I suspect my boss wanted to see if this single mama could really handle being called out on short notice—on her sixth day on the job, no less. This would be the beginning of a four-year Road Runner–Wile E. Coyote relationship.

Often, she would ask me to stay late or come in early when it wasn't really necessary. It was almost as though she was doing everything in her power to force me to use my son as an excuse for not pulling through in my assignments. From time to time, she'd ask me, "How do you do it?" Once, when I'd returned from a 6 P.M. live shot after a nearly ten-hour workday, looking forward to a week-long vacation, she told me I'd have to stay late to back up another reporter on his story, just in case he needed me. It was

Staying a Step Ahead in the Work Game

❋ Make a list of all your babysitter options for all times of the day.

❋ Prioritize the list with names of those who are easiest to access on top.

❋ Ask friends and family to be "on call" for you, and keep their pager numbers with you at all times.

❋ Find resources near your children's school, recreation centers, special teachers, teachers' aides, parents of your kids' friends, and your own friends who can pick the kids up if they're sick or if they miss the bus.

❋ Partner with other single mothers who work different shifts so you can bail one another out.

❋ If Daddy lives nearby, put him in the network.

❋ From time to time, buy your helpers a bag of groceries or make them a special dish to show them how much you appreciate their help.

❋ Have backup plans if your kids lose or forget their house key. Give a key to an elderly neighbor you trust and can count on to be home, or ask the neighbor to hide an unlabeled key to your house somewhere near their house.

❋ Routinely drill your child on all backup plans.

❋ Keep your plan to yourself; coworkers will be amazed at how smoothly you run your life.

absolute nonsense. But she was the boss, and she had the power, as abusive as I felt it was. She and I both knew it was bull, and yet the charade of testing my loyalty to the company had to be played out.

During light-load times at work, my boss would come over to me with an artificial smile and ask how Winston was doing or ask who took care of him during the day. Once she even said, "Well, you know, Kelly, if you ever need my help, I'd be happy to babysit." Right. Like I really wanted my untrustworthy boss to spend time with my kid. She was a real trip.

I talked to my son about it a lot, so he'd understand why I was sometimes later picking him up from the babysitter's than he expected. I wanted him to know that I was as disappointed as he was that I wasn't able to spend extra time with him. Once, when he was about eight years old, I came home pissed. "What's the matter," he said, "Is the boss messin' with the woman?" I always called myself "the woman."

It took more than four years of working under her crazy dictatorship and a lot of complaints from fellow workers about their own issues with the boss before she finally got the axe. It was the best thing that ever happened to my career.

9

School

Another challenge I had not anticipated was the one I faced at Winston's school. Every school in America is a reflection of the people it serves. Many teachers in American schools stereotype single mothers. Unfortunately, many single mamas have not done much to change the stereotype. But to me, that's no excuse.

Children of single mamas are disproportionately labeled "special needs" kids. Too often they're placed in special education classes. Their normal age-appropriate behavior problems may be mis-diagnosed as behaviors linked to attention deficit disorder (ADD). Often our kids' guidance counselors will recommend that they be seen by doctors who routinely prescribe medication for hyperactivity.

As a single mama, you must make sure you're doing everything you can to ensure that your child has every educational advantage possible. Be extra vigilant. See that your child eats well-balanced meals and is not overexposed to television. Make sure he or she gets a good night's sleep, at least eight hours, closer to twelve if he or she is under the age of eight. Give your child enough attention. Provide a calming enviornment close to bedtime.

Medication

If after you do all you can, the guidance counselor still thinks your kid needs to be on medication, get a second opinion. Many pediatricians believe that putting a child on medication for behavior modification is copping out. There's a concern in the medical community about overmedicating children and exposing them to the risk of being dependent on these drugs for life. Do not let any professional make you feel so guilty about being a single mama that you're easily persuaded the drug can somehow take the place of Daddy.

Avoid Labeling

The worst thing you can do is to allow your children to become labeled early in their school career. Early labels are often very hard to shake. "Special ed" kids are looked on by their peers and teachers as problem children, and the kids carry the label through high school. It's no wonder these kids are least likely to succeed. We often let teachers pigeonhole our children, leaving them no way out.

Some children may need to be placed in special classes. If this happens to your child, put a plan together as quickly as you can. Always work with the counselors on a way to make the placement temporary. One of your goals should be mainstreaming your children. Your child may have a physical or mental impairment that keeps him or her behind the pack. Still, give him or her hope for doing better.

If your children are labeled, you must go out of your way to fight for them. If school starts earlier than your workday, drop in sometimes or volunteer to help the teacher. Most teachers love parent volunteers so much, they'll probably be extra nice to your kids—at least while you're there.

Communicate with your children's teachers regularly. Write them notes, letting them know you know what's going on in the classroom. Ask them to send you notes or give you a call at home. Make yourself accessible. Don't be on a high horse when it comes to

Checklist for School

✳ Keep in touch with teachers.
✳ Check backpacks and folders every night.
✳ Review your children's school day.
✳ Have homework rules.
✳ Reward good behavior.
✳ Make sure kids have a good night's sleep.
✳ Have breakfast as a family.

your kids. Give your children's teachers your work, home, and pager numbers, so they can reach you whenever they have some time to give you a call. Understand that your children's teachers have lives, too. So ask them to call you late at night, after 9 P.M., when the children are in bed. The better your relationship with your children's teachers, the better the teachers will relate to your children.

Your pursuit of a good relationship with your children's teachers, especially when there's a paper trail (keep copies), will give you ammunition you may need in the event the teacher and your child are not a good match, and you want to get him or her into another classroom. Getting a child switched to another class is next to impossible in many public schools. Schools have ironclad rules to keep certain teachers from building fan clubs. It makes sense not to mess with the system unless you know your son's or daughter's teacher simply hates your child.

Every day, no matter how tired you are, check your children's backpacks to see if they've done their homework, or if they've brought home something you need to sign. Talk to your children about what happened during their day. Learn each teacher's system, so you'll know when something's not right. Have rules for when your kids will get their homework done. This will build strong, self-directed study habits and foster a desire in your children to learn and do well in school. If your kids are successful in school, they'll have a better chance at being successful in life.

My son tells me positive feedback helps. He says he's encouraged to do well in school when I tell him as many "good" things as "bad" things about my impressions of how he's dealing with school. Finally, he's admitted that a good night's sleep helps him to stay focused the next day. I've found that a good breakfast, especially one I share with him, gets him off to an upbeat start.

Sonya and D-Two

Sonya was doing all the right things when it came to getting her son, D-Two, prepared for kindergarten. She'd taken him to see his classroom before the first day of school. She got him excited about the bus ride. She bought him new clothes and went on and on about what a big boy he was. D-Two was ready for school, and Sonya was confident he would be a successful student.

About two weeks into the school year, Sonya sensed something was wrong. D-Two was losing that sparkle in his eye. When Sonya picked him up from the sitter's after school, his head was hanging low, and he was quieter than usual.

"What's wrong, D-Two?" she'd ask. He'd answer with a comment about how things weren't working out at school. He'd tell his mother he spent time in time-out, or he raised his hand and the teacher wouldn't pick him, or he got in trouble for not standing still in line. Soon, D-Two started bringing home notes about the things he'd been telling his mother about.

Sonya scheduled a conference with D-Two's teacher. She let her know how interested she was in making her son's first year of school a good, healthy one, that would set him on the right track. Sonya provided all her telephone numbers for the teacher to use at any time—her home, work, cell, and pager numbers.

After about a week, things seemed to be looking up. But the next week, it was back to the same old thing. Unfortunately, about this same time, Sonya was dealing with a crisis at work. One of her coworkers had been trying to undermine her performance, setting her up as an incompetent employee. It culminated in a shouting match, where the coworker accused Sonya of babysitting for another employee's fourteen-year-old son at work. Sonya had

---

When the Teacher Doesn't Get It

❋ Give your children the benefit of the doubt, but be open minded.

❋ Stay in constant contact with the teacher.

❋ Volunteer in the classroom.

❋ If you see no improvement, get the principal involved.

❋ Put problems in writing and cc the principal.

❋ Be a tutor to your child or arrange to get help from a high school kid.

❋ Be professional and kind in your dealings with teachers so that you don't become the problem.

❋ Learn your rights from school policy manual about switching teachers.

---

allowed the boy to sit at her desk while his dad was working. But she had no reason to have to go on the defensive for this. That night, when Sonya went home to put what was going on in a memo to send to her boss, she remembered that she had not looked into D-Two's backpack that evening. To her amazement, Sonya discovered a stack of notes the teacher had written. Each was for some minor offense, the kind of thing you'd expect from a five-year-old. It was clear to Sonya that her son annoyed the teacher. Sonya found herself writing two letters that night—one to her boss, the other to her son's principal. The one to the principal requested that her child be moved out of his classroom into another. Both letters were effective. D-Two got a new teacher, and Sonya got the coworker off her back. Sonya's little boy was back to his old self in no time. By the end of the term, he had near perfect grades for his schoolwork and conduct.

Winston

It didn't take long for me to realize my son didn't like his new school in St. Petersburg.

"How was your first day?" I asked. Winston was in the second semester of kindergarten.

"Okay."

"How was the work?"

"Easy."

"How 'bout the kids?"

"Not good. Some are racists."

I was stunned. He and I had just completed watching a lot of news coverage surrounding the 1992 presidential election. We'd discussed a lot of adult topics, including racism, but I'd never heard him refer to anyone as a racist.

"Why do you say that?" I asked.

"Because every time Carter sees me, he calls me Blackie and some of the other kids just laugh."

"What do you do when that happens?"

"Tell the teacher. But she doesn't do anything."

The following week, I met with the teacher. She told me Winston was having some problems adjusting to his new school. She also told me she was very surprised to hear Winston tell her some of the children were racists.

I told her that Winston had shared with me the same story he'd shared with her about the kids. I told her that from his explanation, he was right. The kids were displaying mean, ignorant, racist behavior that hurt my son. The teacher told me she thought Winston was overreacting. She thought it was an "unusual" reaction from a six-year-old, and she suggested that Winston might be trying to get attention, since he was in a new place and away from his father.

I explained to the teacher that Winston had been living with me since he was a baby, and that he lives with his father and stepmother during summers and holidays. I also mentioned that he'd just returned from spending two weeks with them. I told her Winston is one of the most self-assured, secure children she will ever meet.

Holding my anger in, knowing that expressing it could be counterproductive, I suggested she flip her stereotype coin and see the other side. Then she might notice that my child is not the problem. Certainly his status as the child of a single mama had

> ## *Public School or Private School?*
>
> If I had to generalize, I would say that public education is more suited for children of single mamas. However, recent studies say that of all schools, Catholic schools have the best track record for educating inner-city kids.
>
> Single mamas must be aware of everything that their children go through in school. You must ask questions and do your own homework so that youc an put your children in an environment where they will be challenged academically and nurtured socially.

absolutely nothing to do with how he took charge of a situation no child should ever be subjected to. I asked her how she would react if she was a new kid in a school where she was only one of two African-American children and subjected to racist behavior by children from whom she was trying to win approval.

Things improved, but only because the teacher was probably terrified of me. The reason I didn't move Winston to another school or another classroom was that he'd already been dealing with enough change, and I knew "rescuing" him would not be in his best interests.

I eventually switched Winston to a public school with a diverse student and teacher population. So far, so good. He's been an A student in gifted classes. His test scores are in the ninety-ninth percentile of his grade level. He loves learning, and he's popular among his peers and teachers. I spend as much time as I can in Winston's classroom. I enjoy the kids knowing who I am, and I speak to his class about my career whenever possible to let Winston know I'm proud to be a part of his life.

10

Raising Young Black Men

Another reason single mamas rush to get a man in their lives is the whole role-model thing. People are constantly telling us the importance of exposing our children, especially the boys, to positive male role models. We hear about it on TV and read about it in the paper.

We hear stories about little boys whose lives were changed for the better by men in the Big Brothers program or by a basketball coach or a minister at church.

I think it's extremely important for our boys to be exposed to positive African-American men. The best bet is to make these role models men with whom we have no intimate relationships. That way, the relationship can be far more secure and lasting.

Your boys will meet men at church, school, the recreation center, or in the neighborhood; they'll be Boy Scout leaders, choir directors, and Little League coaches. But that doesn't mean they'll all be good role models.

Be Careful

We live in a day and time when it seems that more perverts are on the loose. I've heard and read too many stories about desperate single mamas who trusted every man who showed interest in their

---

Is He a Pervert?

With the advent of Megan's Law, some states force convicted sex offenders to register. In Florida, for example, sex offenders must register with their local newspaper and police station. All of this information is public record. Find out what your state does, and take advantage of this information to check out anyone who will be involved with your children.

---

children. This sets your boys up for the possibility of pain and misery. Imagine what the rest of your boy's life would be like if one of these trusted friends ended up sexually molesting him.

Not long ago, there was a story out of south Florida about a single mama who was befriended by an elderly man. She was so happy that the man had volunteered to help her with the kids. He'd go grocery shopping for the family and invite the kids over to his place when mama had to work. Eventually he was convicted of sexually molesting and murdering one of the children.

You must be careful who you let near your children. People will assume you're needy and vulnerable, so they won't expect you to be cautious and on guard. This is another reason you must be extra alert.

Watch your neighbors. One day, shortly after Winston and I had moved into our new home in St. Petersburg, Winston told me one of our neighbors volunteered to take him with me to the hardware store one day, so he could do something "just for the guys." Winston was just six at the time, but I used that as an opportunity to tell him that although our neighbor was probably just being nice, sometimes bad men pretend to be good just to get boys and girls to trust them. I told him he should never go anywhere without my permission, and no matter how nice a neighbor is, he could be a bad man in disguise. I reminded Winston about "bad men" so much, that by the time he was seven, he told me, "Mom, you think everybody's a pervert." I told him he was right, but that I was only that way because I love him so much and don't want to see him hurt. I reminded him that he should tell me immediately should he feel uncomfortable about anybody in his life.

Relatives, Friends, Neighbors

Your relatives, especially your brothers (if you have them), can be some of the best role models for your boys. Whenever possible, ask them to baby-sit and to involve your sons in their lives. Single mamas who have responsible, trustworthy brothers are very fortunate. Pretty soon, your brothers may love the responsibility so much, you won't have to ask. Your sons should be able to see how men interact with women and how they interact with children. They should get hugs from your brothers, wrestle with them, and just be able to hang with them and observe their actions. Cousins, uncles, and good male friends can be just as wonderful. Just make sure you know and trust them.

Role models may be found in places you'd least expect. One of my son's first role models was the barber. Winston was barely two years old when I'd take him with me to the barbershop. (We had the same haircut back in those days.) I'd give him his apple juice and just sit there with him so he could hear the men talking about boxing and politics. It got to the point where whenever we'd show up, the barber would yell, "Hey Winston, gimme some juice!" By the time Winston was three, I'd drop him off. Of course I'd ask the barber to keep an eye on him, but Winston would always be okay. It made him feel independent, like a big boy. All those men in the shop, in a sense, were role models.

The relationship between a boy and his mother can be strained when there's no "male" outlet. If you're a single mama of boys, go out of your way to make sure your sons have real relationships with men who love them and who'll be a good example for them. Do not let them hang out with anyone you don't want them to emulate. Children are extremely impressionable. They'll pick up the mannerisms, speech, even the body language of the people they're around most.

All kinds of kids get involved in gangs these days, poor, rich, and those of single as well as married parents. (See gang tips in the Other Single Mamas chapter.) Talk to gang bangers, and they'll tell you pretty much the same thing. They were all looking for a family, a place to feel accepted, a place to belong. They were looking primarily for that male feedback. It's amazing how even if the feedback is about something bad that they do well, the boys want to hear it. But ask them, and they'll tell you that given the choice, they would have preferred getting positive feedback for something good they did well. Boys of single mamas are particularly vulnerable to the "thug" life. Mama can only do so much in satisfying her male children's need to feel accepted and to feel like a real young man.

Sports and Clubs

When you look for role models, look for those involved with sports. Being a part of a team can satisfy your boys' male needs to belong and to get approval from guys whom they admire. Every neighborhood has Little League teams or recreation league sports. But this does not mean you should not be involved every step of the way. You'll need to attend your son's games and at least some practices to ensure that the men he is looking up to really deserve his respect and trust. It also sends a red flag to any perverts in disguise that Mom is involved enough to help her child spot trouble. Your involvement will allow you to get to know who's trustworthy and who is not, so that at some point, you can step back a bit and let your son develop the important male relationships he needs.

There are all kinds of clubs your son can join, but sports will probably be the safest outlet, since parents are usually around to watch what's going on. Also check out academic clubs and other group activities offered at museums, churches, and recreation centers. Big Brothers Big Sisters, a program that pairs your son with a man who has volunteered at least one hour a week to be a role model for a boy, is also a good bet. The organization usually does a thorough screening of the men, but here again, always be cautious. The important thing, especially in the beginning, will be your involvement. Make the transition gradual and do all you can to thoroughly check out these programs. The last thing your son needs is to be put into a situation where he trusts a man who ends up letting him down.

Pressure From Others

I admire any single mama who raises a successful African-American man. She has beat the odds and fooled the naysayers. A single mama who has male children will constantly be told what a job she has on her hands. Everywhere she goes, people will be looking for her to slip up.

Men in her life, whether it's her brothers or some man who wants to become attached to her, will be extra tough on her boys. Somehow, bullying the baby will toughen him up, they think. They'll assume your son's "soft," because they'll assume your femininity is rubbing off on him.

I have seen boys who live with no one but their single mama and perhaps their sisters emulate the behaviors of the females they love. It's not that the boy becomes feminine; it's just that he shares the mannerisms of the people he's most often exposed to. Usually that's his single mama and her girlfriends. It doesn't always happen, however, because most boys are exposed to other boys and men. Plus, if the single mama's doing what she should be doing, her sons are spending as much time with their daddy as possible. Where it's impossible, the boys are spending a lot of time with their grand-daddy or the male role models their mothers have carefully selected to help guide their boys' lives.

Communicating With Your Boys

But as a single mama's boys grow older, special challenges will present themselves. Boys will have to talk to someone they trust about things they hear at school about sex and girls. If mama is a healthy communicator, she will often be the confidante of choice. Her sons will ask her questions like, "What's a dick?" or "Are those titties?" You will have to learn how to answer questions like these quickly with a straight face. "A dick is an inappropriate name for a penis. A penis is what you use to go to the bathroom." "Those are breasts. *Titty* is not a good word to use to describe these. They are used to feed babies. Mother cows, dogs, cats—all kinds of female animals—feed their babies the same way." As the boys grow, the questions will become more complicated and more awkward to answer. Being a good single mama means learning how to just answer the question without flinching.

The toughest one for me to date was when Winston asked me out of the blue, "Mom, have you ever used a Trojan latex condom?" All I could say was, "Yes." He was nine years old. Prepare yourselves, single mamas. This, too, shall pass.

No Longer The "Man" of the House

Having male instead of female children is particularly difficult for a single mama when she is dating. The more mistakes you make in the areas we have already explored, the more difficult dating will become. For example, if your child does not spend adequate productive amounts of time with his daddy or some other male role model, he will have an extremely hard time coping when his mama brings a man into the house. He'll most certainly see the man as a direct threat to his position in the family. It is normal for any child of a single mama, male or female, to act out in peculiar ways when faced with the issue of a man and his or her mama. For boys, the new relationship becomes a threat to their maleness. Most say very negative things about the man; they find things not to like about him. Over time, usually when it's too late, they realize the guy wasn't so bad, and they begin to understand how misguided their anger was. By then, the boys have grown up and a lot of harm has already been done.

This problem can be nipped in the bud. The boys must understand early on that this man is not trying to replace their father; he is simply a friend to their mother. Your sons must be allowed to express their feelings openly and honestly. If you see misbehavior that precedes or follows a visit from your friend, sit your son down and have a heart-to-heart talk with him. Let him tell you whatever he's feeling—that he's jealous or afraid or whatever. Hear him out, and constantly reassure him that he's your son and always will be and that no one can replace that relationship.

Raising a Healthy, Happy, Stable Son

* Actively listen when he talks to you.
* Fill his life with love from members of both sexes.
* Do not rescue him from difficult learning situations.
* Let him have a right to his feelings.
* Answer his questions with straight answers.
* Discipline him and give him responsibilities.
* Make him a part of teams (sports, band, scouting).
* Tell him often that you love him.
* Do not ever let him feel anyone has taken him away from you.
* Do not display physical affection for a man in your son's presence until that man is your husband. Even then, be discreet.

Your son should never be referred to by you as your "little man." Any reference to him being in a position that only a man can fill will most definitely make him feel replaced when a real man does come into your life. He's your son, your big boy, and that's it.

Also, if you follow the rules about not letting your children sleep in your bed or stay up all hours of the night, you'll limit the problem of having your son feel displaced. I think it is always a no-no to let your children know about a man in your bed, but there will be times when you slip into your bedroom. If your son feels that's his place, you'll have hell to pay.

John and Antwon

John knew that he had to give back something to his community. He had just joined the sports staff at a big newspaper, and was well aware of the kinds of problems boys face when they do not have positive role models in their lives. He decided to join Big Brothers to do his part to help. His little brother, Antwon, was only seven or eight when they met. His mother was single and had her hands full with three girls as well as her niece and nephew. Antwon's father was in and out of jail. Most of the men in Antwon's 'hood who were doing well were making their money from drugs. You've heard the story before.

Antwon was nervous when he first met John. He really didn't know what to think of this man who wanted to take him to the movies. But he knew it was going to be fun getting out of his small apartment with his mama and sisters and cousins. Turns out they had a great time. When Antwon went to school that Monday, he told all his friends about his weekend experience, and he even shared the story with his teacher. He felt so proud that this big-time guy who lived in a nice house and drove a cool car was going to be his big brother.

As the years passed, not much changed around Antwon's neighborhood. His mother had another baby; some of the boys Antwon had been looking up to ended up getting locked up; Antwon's daddy was still in jail. But there was always someone Antwon could look up to, someone who gave him a kind of hope for the future that a lot of the boys he knew didn't have. John would always come to pick him up, to take him to the library or to the movies or to a nice restaurant.

Antwon never liked school as much as John wanted him to. But he always tried, because he knew John would always ask about his grades, and would sometimes even talk to his teachers. Antwon did whatever he could to impress John.

Children of single mamas need all the parenting they can get, because quite frankly, we can't always be there. It is important to involve your children in the lives of adults who have their best interests at heart. For boys, having a man to provide structure and support in their lives on a consistent basis is so important.

Whenever Antwon has problems in school, John's there to hear what happened and to offer Antwon suggestions for how to improve. Antwon knows John cares about him and is counting on him to do his best. It's that extra added pressure that keeps Antwon on track. He knows his mother might be too busy to really hear

---

Sources for Role Models

* Churches
* Big Brothers or Big Sisters programs
* Community centers
* Fraternities
* Men's groups
* Businesses in your community
* Newspapers (often they have records of stories they've done on role models)

---

what's happening in situations where he gets into trouble, but John has the time. In many ways, John has become a disciplinarian for his "little brother." He lets Antwon know when he's disappointed in him, and he tells him that he expects him to do his best.

It doesn't hurt that John has a steady job, and that he provides a real model for Antwon to see what kind of man he can become when he grows up. In many ways, John is giving Antwon what he would have gotten from his father in an ideal world.

Big Ant'

One of my strongest support systems while I was in Jacksonville was the Johnson family. Miss Barbara was one of the women who worked at the after-care at Winston's school. I must admit that before I met her, I felt a tinge of jealousy every time Winston mentioned her name, which was interesting because until then I'd never been jealous of a woman in Winton's life. I suspected Miss Barbara was white, and that made me feel even more uneasy about my son's adoration for this woman.

One day I had to pick Winston up early, and Miss Barbara and I finally met face to face. Her hours were 1 P.M. to 5 P.M., so she was always gone when I came for Winston at the usual hour of 6 P.M. As I approached the auditorium, I saw for the first time at Riverside

---

Other Kids' Daddies Make Good Role Models

Include in your children's circle of friends nuclear families where the dad's involved with his kids. If you don't, and your children only see their father on weekends and holidays, they'll be deficient in their knowledge of how a father is supposed to function. Only through example will your children learn how mothers and fathers who live under the same roof interact with each other and their children. Do not be threatened if, at times, your children feel more comfortable with their "other family" than they do at home with you. It's only natural that they should feel comfortable. In an ideal world, a home where children live with Mom and Dad is natural, and it's only natural that at times your children will crave that kind of home.

Presbyterian Day School a black face, other than the one belonging to my son. I wondered who she was.

"Hi, Mommy," Winston said when he saw me enter the auditorium.

Then the black woman I'd spotted earlier came up behind him. "Here's his jacket," she said, smiling.

"Oh, thanks. I'm Kelly Williams, Winston's mother."

"Hi, I'm Barbara."

"Oh, Miss Barbara, I've heard a lot about you. Winston talks about you all the time."

As Winston and I headed home across the bridge, I was relieved to have met Miss Barbara. And as racist as this sounds, I was glad she was black. Somehow I thought Winston's feelings about this woman meant I was doing a good job building my son's self-identity and self-esteem.

Getting settled into Jacksonville was easier than I thought it would be. And Miss Barbara, her husband, Big Ant', and son, Little Anthony were a big help; they ended up becoming part of my new extended family. In many ways, Big Ant' was a role model to my son. He was a black man in his home with his family, who taught Winston how to fish, how to play catch, and how to share.

Winston began to spend more time with Big Ant' when I started free-lancing at the television station. He'd go fishing with him and just hang out with Big Ant' and his friends. Big Ant' told him how to defend himself against Little Ant' when Little Ant' would harass him or take a toy from him.

Big Ant' also taught Winston how to play basketball and Uno. Simply by being there for his wife and child, Big Ant' modeled for Winston what a husband and family man is. Winston had really never seen that, outside my family when he spent time with my parents. Big Ant' was neither a rich man nor a super-educated one, but where it mattered, he was a role model for my son, one who made a lasting impression.

Jerome

Jerome was just a month shy of his seventeenth birthday when I met him. I had agreed to make a presentation at the American Cancer Society's walkathon. It was a weekend in March, and cold for a Florida morning. The people gathered for the walkathon, most of them white and middle aged, were coworkers from various big corporations that had made huge pledges. Some brought their children; other groups were from area churches. But two of the walkers stood out like sore thumbs. They wore baggy khaki pants and hooded fleece sweatshirts at least two sizes too big. Their sneakers were beat up. One covered his head with the hood of his sweatshirt. The shorter one probably should have. His hair was matted, and he looked like he hadn't had a haircut in months.

When I finished my little speech, I joined the two boys and asked them about themselves. We ended up walking together. I learned they were both inmates at a juvenile detention facility and were allowed to go on the outing with a congregation from a church across the street from the facility. They'd been attending regular services there, and the outing was a reward for good behavior.

The boys were Jerome and Mack. Mack, the taller one, was

sixteen. He told me he had lived in a group home in Pensacola for foster children and was locked up for possession of a gun. He told me he'd played hooky from school one day to go to a friend's house to meet some girls. The boy let him play with his father's gun. But Mack decided to hang on to the gun when he went back to school; it was a way to show off. When he and some friends got together near the school to smoke some reefer, the principal caught them and called the police. Mack was caught redhanded with the marijuana and the gun.

Jerome was a tough guy, not as talkative or as trusting as Mack when it came to answering my questions. He, too, was a foster child, and had lived in several homes growing up. He remembered his mother, from whom he'd been separated at age seven. He said she was a crackhead who'd left the house, telling Jerome and his sister she'd be right back. Four days later, when she still had not returned, the authorities showed up to put the kids in the state's care. Jerome's sister was placed with him at first. But later, they went to separate homes.

As I got to know Jerome better, he told me more about his childhood and his parents. He had always been bright, and in the beginning he made good grades in school. But as a foster child, he wore hand-me-down clothes and no one seemed to make a big deal of his good grades. His classmates often teased him about what he wore and about his nappy hair, since no one ever took him to get regular haircuts. Eventually he learned that some of the older, cooler boys would sell crack to make money to buy designer sneakers. They'd often buy them at a discount from other criminals who'd steal clothes from the mall and sell them out of their cars. Jerome did pretty well selling drugs. He started to dress a whole lot better and the kids stopped teasing him at school. Soon he found selling drugs more satisfying than getting A's, so he stopped going to school so much. This landed him in juvenile detention on several occasions. Once, while locked up, he got into a fight with a white boy who claimed to be a neo-Nazi. Jerome decided to prove his manhood to his black and Hispanic friends by beating up the white kid. That's how he'd ended up serving six months at the facility with Mack.

Help for Kids Like Jerome

* Foster Care Independent Living Program—kid must sign up and be recommended by caseworker prior to eighteenth birthday
* Transitional living programs offered by state and church organizations
* In some cities, Salvation Army, Goodwill, and other large homeless shelters have special educational, employment placement services, and living quarters for single young people.
* Some state foster care programs allow older teens to lease space from a foster parent who acts more as a landlord than a full-time parent.

Jerome told me that he'd met his father during the time he was on the street hustling drugs. His father was also addicted to crack. Jerome still had no idea where his mother was, and he claimed he didn't care, but when I pressed him, he admitted he was curious. He was also deeply hurt that she'd abandoned him. One of his memories of her was of a time when her boyfriend lived with them. Apparently this guy was physically abusive to Jerome's mother and at least verbally abusive to Jerome and his sister. Jerome sounded as though he had to compete with this guy for his mother's affection.

When Jerome was released from the juvenile facility, he was turned over to a homeless shelter. By then, he was eighteen, and no longer in the foster care program. I let him stay with us for a while, until I could get him placed in a transitional living facility. Jerome ended up back in trouble for stealing, and later for selling drugs. I have no idea what will become of him; but I'm certain that his lack of a loving mother, father, and male role models had everything to do with his failures. Until I met Jerome, I never knew how important a mother's love is to a boy whose father is not around.

Pam and Justin

Justin was doted on wholly and completely by his single mama. He was the kind of son anyone would want—friendly, intelligent, and athletic. His father bailed out when Justin was about five years old, so his mama did all she could to make up for the loss. She became Justin's supermama. She took him to all of his practices for all the sports he played; she made all the games, too. She dropped in at school whenever she could, which was often. She wanted to make sure her son wanted for nothing.

Justin had in many ways become Pam's little buddy. They'd talk and laugh and watch movies together. Justin rarely slept in his own bed. Why should he? There was a pillow and plenty of good room in his mama's bed. Most of the time, Pam was too tired to wake Justin and move him into his own bed. Plus, the company was nice.

The only thing Justin really did not have that he needed was his dad. His father was one of those men single mamas love to hate. He left Justin's mama and moved on to his single life without looking back. He had no idea what a wonderful child he'd left behind.

That's one of the reasons Pam became so excited when she met Mark. He was everything her ex was not. He was considerate, respectful, and honest. When he said he was going to do something, she knew he'd come through. He always did.

When Mark would come to visit, he'd put up with the interruptions from Justin and the little boy's constant plays on his mother's emotions to get her attention. He'd even do what he could to make Justin feel included. He'd spend time trying to help him do his homework, anything to make sure Justin did not feel left out. He'd attend his games and even take him to the movies or to McDonald's every now and then.

But Mark could not get close enough to Pam. Whenever the two of them would watch television in her bedroom, Justin would join them. He'd lie right down on his side of the bed, where he always did.

Eventually Mark raised the issue with Pam. She told Mark she couldn't ask Justin to sleep in his own bed, because she'd never done that before and Justin would feel Mark was taking his place. This seemed all right with Mark for a while, but it became such a

Get That Boy Out of Your Bed

I used to have a problem with children sleeping with their parents. I've always thought that after the first few weeks of a child's life, the baby needs to be in his own bed.

I'm now a bit more flexible. In a two-parent household, it's probably all right to let baby sleep with Mom and Dad for a couple of months and every once in a while after that. But for single mamas, this is a no-no.

This is especially true when you're the single mama of a son. The older your boy gets, the more unhealthy his sleeping with you will seem. Your boy is not your man. He's your child. If you let him get into the habit of sleeping in your bed, you will have to deal with all kinds of issues when it's time to put him out. The rejection is something some boys never get over.

My son used to ask me whether he could sleep in my bed. Sometimes, even at the age of ten, he'll ask if he can lie down with me and watch television. Sometimes I'll let him watch a show with me, but after that, he has to go to his own bed. He understands that my bed is my space. I think both single mamas and their sons sleep better and are better off if they have their own space.

problem after a while that he began distancing himself from Pam emotionally. Pam knew she'd have to talk to Justin.

Justin did not understand his mother's meanness. He hated not being next to her in that big warm bed. He could not sleep when he was forced into his own bed. He wanted his mama.

Soon he found a solution. Every night, he'd take his pillow from his bed and put it outside his mama's door. He'd curl up and whimper until he finally fell asleep. This went on for two years, long after Pam and Mark had become husband and wife. And even after Pam and Mark had a daughter, Justin always felt insecure, somehow threatened by his mama's knight in shining armor.

11

Mamas and Daughters

A single mama and her daughter will be friends and foes. Problems may arise because in the back of her mind the single mama will always fear that her daughter will repeat the cycle of single-mamahood, and the single mama will go out of her way to see that it does not happen. Herein will lie unique differences that exist between single mothers and their daughters when there is no man in the house.

Girl Power!

In St. Petersburg, I recently got involved with a program called Girl Power! It's a federally funded campaign to teach girls aged nine through fourteen healthy messages. Its goal is to reduce addictions, pregnancies, suicides, and other destructive behaviors among girls. Most of the girls who attended the first Girl Power! meeting were African American. I noticed that in the brainstorming sessions about what the girls wanted out of the program, many of them giggled and gossiped and didn't seem to take the program very seriously. However, they'd taken a lot of care with their nails, hair, and outfits. It took me back to my junior high school and high school days when I noticed most of my peers put far more emphasis on outward appearance than on their studies. In both cases, I learned, many of these girls were daughters of single mamas.

When I spoke to the girls during a pep talk, I told them my definition of "healthy." Healthy means exercising and eating right, and I let them know that I think taking care of your mind is also an important part of being healthy. I told them a healthy state of mind is feeling so good about yourself that when a boy compliments your beauty, you should be able to say, "Yeah, I know that. Tell me something I don't know." Healthy, positive self-awareness is something that we, as single mamas, must instill in our daughters. The hard part is that often *we* never felt that good about ourselves. It may be why you're in the boat you're in now. Even with my sense of self, I know I've fallen for my share of weak lines from men and ended up where I shouldn't have as a result. To break the cycle, we have to learn how to reinforce the positive with our girls.

A single mama must be honest with her daughters. She must remember that her daughters are not mini versions of herself. They are little girls who should have the same advantages you'd provide for boys.

Daddy's Girl

It is as equally important for your daughters as for your sons to have their fathers in their lives. If your daughters' father is not alive, remind them of who their daddy was and how he felt about his little girls. If their daddy is alive, do everything in your power to facilitate a healthy relationship between Daddy and his daughters.

I have felt for a long time that girls who become pregnant at an early age are searching for love in all the wrong places. I've heard too many single mamas make disparaging remarks to their little girls. "Get your little nappy-headed self over here, girl!" "Girl, where you goin' with them ashy legs?" "You need to eat with your skinny self"—nasty remarks that you wouldn't make to your worst enemy. Meantime, there's no father figure around to tell the girl what daddies should tell their daughters. She never hears her father say, "You look so beautiful today." "Four A's and one B. That's my girl." "You're going to grow up to become a pilot."

Too often the first time the daughter of a single mama hears something positive about herself is when she's twelve years old, and a boy says, "Girl, you are so fine with your cute ass." She's so eager to hear that good stuff again that she's willing to do anything—and I mean anything—to make it happen. So she allows herself to be seduced, and the cycle continues.

Talk to Your Daughters

So mama, if you have daughters, pay attention to their feelings. Involve your girls in all kinds of activities, sports, music, whatever they seem interested in. Spend lots of time with the girls and let them talk about and share their feelings. Hear your daughters out, no matter how difficult their questions become. Be honest with them. There's nothing more disappointing to a girl than to learn her mama lied to her.

Eventually the issue of your single status will come up. Your daughter will ask you whether you were married when you got pregnant or if you were married when she was born; she may even ask you whether you were a virgin when you had sex with her dad. If you're ashamed of your answer to these kinds of questions, so be it. Shame should not preclude you from answering the questions honestly. Tell your little girl, "Yes, I got pregnant when I was not married.... I was not as secure and smart as you are. I thought by having sex with a boy, I'd be able to have him love me for the rest of my life. I wasn't like you are. I didn't realize the most important person for me to love was myself. I'm glad I have you. But I did not do the right thing." Only by being honest about what you've done in the past will your daughters respect you and learn to make the right kinds of decisions for themselves.

Why Is He Here?

Daughters, like sons, will be threatened by the presence of a man in your life. They will resent the time taken away from them to spend with this man. They will cringe at the sight of any physical displays between the two of you. They will feel as though this man has moved into their territory. Sometimes, I've even seen girls flirt with their mothers' boyfriends in order to divert attention away from their mamas. Look closely at your daughter's behavior, and use active listening (from the Help! chapter) to find out what's really going on inside her heart. Never look at your daughter as a competitor. If you ever feel threatened by your daughter—that is, if you ever feel as though you're in competition with her—explore the problem from all sides. If, after honest dialogue and even counseling you learn the problem is your man's interest in your little girl, get rid of him. He's a pervert, and you don't need him. If you find, on the other hand, that your daughter is manipulating the situation to have you all to herself, take lots of time with her to assure her you're not leaving her for any man, even if he does become your husband.

If you're involved with a man, you should spend extra time with your daughter. Do not force her to feel isolated; she does not deserve that. Plus, you don't want her thinking a man is the answer to all of your prayers. You'll only be sending her the message that all she has to do is to find a man and she'll have it made. Keep the lines of communication open.

A Delicate Balance

Some single mamas tend to go overboard in their displays of love for their daughters. Out of regret, guilt, or fear, they shower their little girls with material things. The daughters learn no matter what happens, "My mama will be there to bail me out." These daughters may break the single-mamahood cycle, but they never really grow up. They have trouble focusing on educational and career goals. They look for someone to come along to give them all the things that mama gave them. They are afraid to venture out on their own, because they've never had to.

Some single mamas push their daughters toward beauty pageants, modeling, cheerleading, and other activities that reward girls' physical beauty. I'm not totally against these things; they have their place; but don't live out your insecurities about your own beauty through your daughters' lives. Let them make some choices, and help by balancing their activities. There should be a healthy mix of clubs and programs that reward beauty and those that reward creativity, brain power, athletic, and artistic skill. Remember, you want to break the cycle of single mamahood. To do this, your daughters must feel powerful enough to see boys' attempts to get into their panties for what they are. They must learn that to be successful, they must not trade in their goals for a boy's affection.

Single mamas should not forget that girls need lots of hugs and kisses from their mothers. Your daughter should know that loving touches do not have to be sexual. You're her best teacher here. Hold her hand until she tells you she's too old for it. Give her hugs when she needs them and even when she doesn't. Give her lots of kisses and tell her often that you love her and think she's the most incredible girl on the face of the earth.

Preteen years will be tough ones for your girls. Just remember when you were that age. When I think of the support I got from my mother during my junior high school days, I am convinced it's the only reason I survived. I'd come home from school in tears. I just knew I was the ugliest, skinniest, most flat-chested teenager in the whole world. My mother knew what I was going through. I don't know how many nights she'd come into my bedroom to hold me and tell me I was beautiful and smart and incredible. She told me she knew I was having a hard time, but that things would get better. She promised.

Be there for your daughters. Let them know you'll listen to them. But do not always rescue them. Let your girls make mistakes. Remember, that's how you learned a lot of what you know. Above all, let them become the individuals that they are. Do not hamper the blossoming of your flowers by trying to shape and mold them into the flower you wish you had become.

Tell your daughter over and over again that beauty comes in many shapes and sizes. Encourage her to eat balanced meals that are loaded with fresh fruits and vegetables. Be a role model for her when it comes to physical fitness. Take walks or jogs with her. Tell her over and over again that she's smart and beautiful and talented. Make her believe it.

Tips for Raising a Strong Daughter

* Read to her when she's a baby and throughout early childhood.

* Hold her hand, hug her, and kiss her.

* Don't call her names.

* Always encourage her to do right, and reward good behavior.

* Be honest with her.

* Never treat her differently from her brothers.

* Get her involved in sports.

* Give her responsibilities.

* Praise her when she does well.

* Respect her opinions.

* Constantly tell her you love her.

* Talk to her the way you wish your mama would have talked to you.

* Partner her with a close, trustworthy female friend of yours.

Martha and Tayisha

Martha was only fourteen when she became pregnant. She was fifteen when Tayisha was born. Martha's mama was always cold and distant. She never told Martha anything about sex, except that if you have feelings for a boy, you need to pray. As a result, Martha spent a lot of time when she was thirteen and fourteen trying to figure out what all the mystery was about. She got a lot of attention from the boys that she simply could not get at home from her mama, and she spent a lot of time begging for mercy.

Martha's mama was single, and her daddy lived across town. She'd call her daddy and see him whenever she could. But Martha's mama discouraged this relationship. Martha's daddy had remarried, and Martha's mama did not like her ex's wife or their children.

Martha always had to sneak to see her daddy, in the same way she sneaked to see the boys who'd make her feel so loved. When she got pregnant, her secret of sneaking around and lying to see boys was revealed. Martha's mama never said a thing about the pregnancy. After the baby was born, she suggested Martha drop out of school and work at the supermarket. Fortunately one of Martha's teachers had told her about a daycare for teen moms, and she advised Martha to finish school and plan to go to college to make something of herself. She also told Martha things she's never heard from her mama—that she was beautiful and smart and destined for success.

Martha ended up finishing college and becoming a human resources manager for a major corporation. Her daughter, Tayisha, outgoing and smart, was growing up to become quite a young lady. She was involved in a lot of activities, including ballet, jazz dancing, violin lessons, Girl Scouts, and a church youth group. Martha wanted to do everything in her power to see that Tayisha did not become a single mama, herself.

"Mama, why are we always going places? Why can't we just go home after school?" Tayisha asked her one day.

"Well, Tayisha, I just don't want you to meet a boy when you're fifteen and get married and leave Mommy," she answered dishonestly. She explained that if Tayisha was involved in a lot of activities, she would be less likely to want to "get married," because she'd have other goals and dreams.

Martha would ignore any signs that Tayisha was missing something by not seeing her father. She told Tayisha that it was best that she not be involved with her father, because he was having some problems. Actually Martha had moved away from the town where Tayisha's father lived after the relationship between the two of them became strained. She wanted Tayisha's father out of her life so badly that she never considered what his absence would do to Tayisha.

When Tayisha was fifteen, Martha began to have strange feelings about what was going on in her daughter's life. She suspected something wasn't quite right, but she was afraid to confront her suspicions head on. Then one day, Martha called Tayisha's school and asked to speak to her. She was told Tayisha was not there. "What do you mean she's not there?" Martha demanded. Within minutes, Martha was at the school, scouring the campus, looking for her daughter.

After about an hour-long search, Tayisha showed up in the gymnasium. She had no explanation for why she had not attended class. Martha walked Tayisha back to her classroom and instructed her to get on the bus after school and go straight home.

When Martha arrived at her apartment that evening, something froze her in her tracks at the front door. For whatever reasons, she could not bring herself to turn the key. She had an eerie feeling and knew something was wrong.

Martha went next door to ask her neighbor to come with her into the apartment. Her neighbor actually entered the apartment first. What they found was Tayisha lying on the kitchen floor unconscious with her wrist slit. Martha screamed at the top of her lungs. Someone caled 911, and within minutes the paramedics were there. Fortunately Tayisha had not lost much blood.

At the hospital, Martha learned why Tayisha had tried to take her own life: "I just wanted to kill myself because I knew you'd kill me if you found out about me."

"Found out what, Tayisha?"

"That I'm pregnant."

Martha arranged for her daughter to have an abortion. She transferred Tayisha to another school and asked her to just forget all about what had happened. It was the past, she said.

At a new school, things got off to a pretty good start, but Tayisha was never quite the same. She was always bright, but never focused.

By the time Tayisha was twenty-six, she still had not completed college, was only working part time, and was suffering from depression. She told her psychiatrist that she'd felt trapped ever since she was fifteen.

She said her mother never allowed her to talk about how she felt about not having her father in her life. Whenever she raised the

---

Moving From the Wrong Road to the Right One With Your Daughter

* Acknowledge your mistakes.

* It's never too late to start telling her you love her.

* Try to talk to your daughter at the first signs of "distancing."

* If she won't talk, seek counseling.

* If possible, get Daddy involved; if not, try Granddaddy or an uncle she respects.

---

topic, her mom would get angry or change the subject. Tayisha felt she needed answers to questions about her father, but her mother offered none.

The psychiatrist said Tayisha had become very promiscuous because she was looking for love. He said she had tried to talk to her mother about what she was going through, but was unsuccessful.

Sadly, Martha became defensive and angry when the psychiatrist shared this information. She said her daughter was old enough to know right from wrong, and that her father's absence and Martha's refusal to discuss it had nothing to do with Tayisha's troubles.

Ten years later, Martha feels guilty and angry and will not take any of the responsibility for the strained relationship that she and Tayisha have.

12

Finances

Money is the crucial factor that comes between a single mama and her children's father more often than any other. Taking care of children can create a huge financial hardship. In fact, money is a stumbling block in a lot of areas when it comes to single mamahood. It can be at the root of rationalizing an unhealthy affair with the wrong man; the reason a single mama has a tough time deciding where to draw the line when it comes to work and home; and too often the reason there's so much stress in a single-mama-headed home.

Once you determine you're going to become a single mama, seek child support. Depending on where you live, doing so can be a huge hassle or a fairly simple procedure. County attorneys sometimes have special child support task forces; women's organizations and welfare departments can steer you to public resources available to single women who need to collect child support. If you can afford an attorney, get one, but be careful. There are a lot of bloodsucking lawyers out there ready to pounce on a vulnerable single mama who's so desperate to get revenge against her ex that she'll pay anything for it.

Your best bet with child support is to start early. Many states allow women to file for chld support while they are pregnant; you can even request partial payment for your prenatal expenses. If you have no resources, use whatever free services are available, but be patient and persistent. Because you are sharing lawyers with a whole lot of other single mamas, you'll often have to wait your turn. Put money away, even if it's just a few dollars a week. Live your life as though you have no child support coming, even after you start collecting, because you never know whether your ex will always be employed.

Starting the process early requires that you have the mindset I've spoken of in earlier chapters. You must think of yourself as a single mama. Once again, do not put off collecting child support for fear that you'll hurt and anger the man who was once the man of your dreams. If he really had been your prince, you wouldn't have to go after him now for child support. He would already have you set up, and you would be getting checks on a regular basis, without having to ask for the money. Do not feel guilty about collecting what rightfully belongs to your child. There are too many single mamas out there saying, "I didn't even go after child support. I didn't need the bastard." The problem with that attitude is that you're taking away from your child. Child support is not about you. Remove your heart from the picture, and think with your head. The last time you thought with your heart, you didn't get far. Your kid deserves better.

Above all else, keep your cool. Do not let your heart rule your head. States have guidelines for properly collecting child support. It's not something you'll get rich from; it's intended to allow your children to have the financial resources they are entitled to.

Before I say more about child support, let me make one thing perfectly clear: Child support is for your kids, not for you. If you lose sight of this, you risk making some very bad decisions. There are so many women who will not attempt to collect child support in the beginning of their single mamahood because somehow they feel guilty; they think they're imposing on their ex. Typically, these are the single mamas-to-be and single mamas who still think they have a chance with their children's fathers. They're afraid that by raising the issue of child support, they'll never have a chance to get their man. These women use all kinds of excuses about why they don't want to seek support. "Well, he gives me money for the baby." "He buys me

It's Not Fair

There's nothing fair about child support. Two men who make the same amount of money and have the same number of kids will often pay two different amounts. Although states have guidelines and formulas, judges decide how much each father or mother should pay the custodial parent.

Your best bet is not to get bent out of shape if your girlfriend is getting more support than you are. Just be concerned about your situation and your children.

If you know you've made out like gangbusters and you've left your ex in the poorhouse, be considerate when it comes to your children's needs. If you can afford to send the kids to Daddy's for Christmas, and you know he cannot pay for them to come, don't be stingy. Do not make your kids suffer. They had nothing to do with this, and above all, they did not ask to be born.

groceries." "He gives me gas money." All those things are well and good, but child support is a different story: it provides your children what they'd have financially if Daddy was there with you to help raise them. When you first bring up the issue of child support, or when your ex is first served papers to appear in court, expect him to get upset and emotional and to try to change your mind. If he knows how badly you want him to marry you, he'll really become manipulative. Be prepared, listen to what he has to say, but stick to your guns.

There is an irony around the issue of child support: I've talked to so many men who got angry when the issue was first raised but who now appreciate that they pay child support. They're proud that they've been able to live up to their responsibility. As a result, they're more regular about seeing their children—some of them even respect their kids' single mamas more. Somehow, the extra income takes enough stress and strain off the single mama to let her respect herself more, too.

Child support is not punishment for what Daddy may have done to hurt you in the past—it's his responsibility. If you earn a good living and he does not, make sure he can still afford to visit the kids or have them visit him. I know too many men who live from paycheck to paycheck and often have to take out a loan to see their children. In every one of these cases, the mother is doing nothing to help.

Don't Count Your Chickens Before...

While you're waiting to receive child support, be conservative about spending. Do not go out and rent an expensive apartment or put money down on an expensive car or house, expecting that by the time the bills come in, you'll be receiving your child support check. Nine times out of ten, it won't be that easy. I have yet to talk to a single mama who tells me her child support came in when she expected it.

Even after you begin to receive child support, there will likely be some unexpected expenses. As your children grow, they'll eat more. You'll need to buy a lot more groceries. Plus, because of your time constraints, you'll be forced to eat out a lot. Those trips to Burger King and Pizza Hut will add up faster than you know, not to mention what harm the extra grease and fat will do to your family's health.

Your children's taste in clothes will change. They'll be asking you to buy all kinds of designer styles that cost more than *your* designer stuff. Be careful here—you don't have to give your children everything they want.

If your kids are preteens and teenagers, encourage them to work a few hours a week on a part-time job. They can deliver newspapers or babysit. If you live in an urban area, they may be able to bag groceries or bus tables in a restaurant. Rural or suburban kids can make a few extra bucks doing yard work. As long as your child's work is safe, moral, and legal, and it's not taking away from his or her studies, it can be a big help financially. Plus, it teaches kids about responsibility and the importance of saving.

Once your kids get involved in sports and other activities, you'll find yourself spending money on things like uniforms, fees, and out-of-town trips for competitions. You'll end up buying ice skates and dance outfits that can only be worn one time or a few times until your kids grow into a new size.

Speaking of parties, don't forget to budget expenses for Halloween costumes and trick-or-treating, Thanksgiving company, and Christmas. If you have no children, these days can be treated like other days, but there's no way they'll go unnoticed (unless it's against your religion to celebrate them) if you're a single mama.

Having children means having added wear and tear on your house. Things will get broken. Your kids or their friends will flush stuff down the toilet that does not belong down there. They'll spill things on your carpet, despite the many times you tell them not to bring food into the living room. They'll put stuff in the garbage disposal that doesn't belong there either. The walls of your house will need extra cleaning and painting. Dirty hands can destroy a paint job faster than you know.

Kids also dirty up cars, and their messes will mean you'll have to spend extra money at the car wash, or for cleaning materials so you can wash the car yourself. Having children means having to deal with a lot of nasty sticky crap everywhere.

When your children are young, you'll feel obligated to buy them the same toys their friends from two-parent homes have. Bills from all those birthday parties and holidays will add up. As the kids grow, they'll want a computer, video games, a CD player and CDs, a television, even Internet capability. Being a single mama often means being broke.

Money-Saving Tips for Single Mamas

* When your kids are babies, find a nearby consignment shop willing to do trades. You can take in the nicer baby clothes that your kids hardly wore and trade up for bigger sizes.

* Check out consignment shops for yourself. You'd be surprised how many shops sell designer clothing that are brand new, or worn maybe once or twice.

* Look in your Yellow Pages under Consignment Shops. The ones that sell "better clothing" are usually larger and better

organized. After you start shopping and asking around a little, you'll come to know which ones are the best in your area.

＊ Find outlet stores. Big department stores have huge warehouse locations where they send shipments of clothing that was either overstocked or slow to sell in their areas. This does not mean the clothing is of poor quality or ugly. It could mean it was much too upscale, too trendy, or too high-fashion for a store in a certain location. So it's shipped to the warehouse. Find out where these big close-out warehouses are for your favorite department store. Make it a habit to do most of your shopping there. Talk about bargains! You can find designs straight out of your favorite fashion magazines for rock-bottom prices.

＊ Don't buy retail. Single mamas can't afford to be stupid enough to do the retail-never-on-sale thing.

＊ Try not to take younger kids shopping with you. Until your children are around ten years old, it's best to just get to know their taste and pick up their clothes when you're on your own shopping trips. That way, you don't have to hear their whining, and they won't know what they're missing.

＊ Outlet stores are great places to buy your kids' shoes. If possible, get your kids' shoe sizes from the shoes they are currently wearing, and when they are not with you, buy them something similar in a half to a whole size bigger. If the shoes are too big, save them a few months. Once your kids are old enough to sit still and understand that sometimes a favorite shoe is not available in their size or costs too much, you can bring them along on the shopping trip. Otherwise, it's not really worth the trouble.

＊ Pawn shops are great places to shop for household appliances. The larger chain pawn shops usually give you some sort of warranty on larger purchases. You'll get better deals when you buy more than one item. Never pay the asking price.

＊ Those coupons that come in the Sunday paper are a lifesaver for single mamas. You may not need all of them, but the ones for fast food and convenient neighborhood restaurants are worth the trouble of clipping. Keep them in an envelope in your car. They'll come in handy.

Healthcare Deals

Healthcare costs can add up for single mamas, perhaps more than any other unset expense. It's important to select a healthcare plan that is both cost-effective and gives you the choices you and your children need. Make sure you find on your plan a doctor you feel comfortable with who understands the unique needs of a working single mama. That way, you'll be worked in for appointments early in the morning or on the weekend, if weekend hours are available, when your kids are sick. Your doctor should empathize with your plight of having to do three jobs—the one that pays the bills, the mama's and the daddy's. If he or she doesn't have full sympathy and understanding, pick another doctor. Always be pleasant to the receptionist and nurses; this will help you when you're desperate to get your kids to the doctor at a convenient time, and will also keep you from having to use emergency care that your health plan may not cover. By the way, when you're working out your child support package, ask about whether your children can be covered on their father's health plan. If they can, you will save a lot of money.

Long-Term Planning

One of the lessons I learned from my friend Sonya is the importance of estate planning. If at all possible, make sure the daddy has a life insurance plan where your children are the sole beneficiaries. That way, they'll have income from their father in the event that his life ends before they turn eighteen or finish college, or whenever their child support expires. This is something you'll need to discuss with your lawyer. Sonya's husband, David, had life insurance coverage through his job to cover his family's needs. As a result, Sonya's children were able to have the kind of home and life David had worked so hard to provide for his family before his untimely death. Getting the maximum coverage through your job is usually your best bet.

He'll Get Over It

Don't get me wrong. Your concern that you'll make the father of your child mad at you is valid; in fact you can expect him to be angry. But once the man gets over his anger, he'll probably be a much improved father. It's better to make him mad for a little while and to have support in taking care of your kid than it is to have him totally removed from the child's life physically, psychologically, and financially. Put your children first, and do everything you can to make their life secure.

Ask your lawyer to ensure that if your ex discontinues support, his wages will be garnisheed. Of course, if he hides his wages in some sort of corporation, this is next to impossible—but remember, the law is on your side. If he's doing something illegal, chances are it'll catch up with him. If your children's father is the type who gives you your checks in person, be nice. Always thank him. I know that sounds crazy, but the more you make him feel he's acting like a man, the easier it will be to get him to keep his commitment to the kids. I don't care if the man hasn't given you a check in three years and when he finally gives in, under pressure, say "Thank you," and tell him it means a lot to you and it will help a lot with the kids.

Kindness Pays

The surprising thing about fathers and child support is that once all the anger over your seeking and finally collecting money is solved, men sometimes give their children's mother a little extra. I know a lot of single mamas who ask their exes kindly for extra money for special things that come up with the kids; more times than not, the dads who started out resisting paying are more than willing to help out. Again, it's all about letting them know how much you appreciate the money—making them feel they're good fathers who are living up to their responsibility. Just make sure asking for the extra does not create a problem with your ex and his new woman or wife.

I've spoken to several men who never paid child support and never saw their kids, until the children were adults and made it their business to get in touch with their dads. These men told me

---

Single Mamas' Tips For Collecting Child Support

* Understand the rules in your state.
* Seek the maximum allowable for your children.
* Don't agree to anything "under the table."
* Understand the "formula" used to determine what your children need.
* Do everything legally possible to find out his total income.
* File papers with the help of a private attorney or the D. A.'s office.
* Be aggressive.
* If he questions paternity, have the baby tested at birth.
* Don't be intimidated.
* Don't get emotional in court.
* Don't be wishy-washy.
* Don't back down.

---

one of the reasons they avoided contact with the children was the guilt they felt about not paying child support. This was the case whether the men avoided paying support by fighting it or were never pursued for it.

On the other hand, I've spoken to women whose husbands have children from a previous marraige and pay support for them. These women tell me their husbands' strong desire to spend a lot of time with their kids is largely based on the fact that that's where their money is going. These are men who feel more obligated to be with their kids because they know they are financially responsible for seeing that the kids' needs are met. If you're inclined to give up fighting for support for your kids because you think it's just not worth the hassle or because you don't want to make your ex angry, you should remember that once men give to their children, their commitment to them tends to grow stronger.

Take yourself and your ego out of it. Think about your kids and what's right for them. There are a lot more things you can do to ensure that your children are provided for financially by their fathers than you can do to ensure that their dad takes care of them emotionally. You are your kids' advocate. If you can't get them both the financial and psychological support they need from their dad, at least take care of the financial. It is worth the fight.

Child support is not just payment for living expenses, it is also money to help send your children to spend time with dads who live out of town. It's money to help you with private school education, if that's what you and your children's father want for the kids. It's help with daycare, too.

Take your time. Check out the Yellow Pages and talk to friends. Above all else, be patient.

Karrie and Carlton

Karrie was thirty-nine years old and in her third year of law school when she found herself a single mama-to-be. Her beau, Carlton, convinced himself she got pregnant on purpose. Neither he nor Karrie used birth control, because Karrie told him that doctors had told her she was infertile. She believed them, and he believed Karrie, and then suddenly one day she was expecting.

To say Karrie was poor is an understatement. She had a part-time job and faced eighty thousand dollars in law-school loans. She now needed Carlton more than ever, but he felt nothing but the urge to get out of Dodge City. Already, Carlton had two children, with two different women, and he'd convinced himself each of those single mamas also got pregnant on purpose—to keep him, of course.

Karrie wanted to keep her child. She'd never been married, but she had been pregnant twice when she was much younger. Each time she chose to have an abortion. She always regretted not keeping those children, especially after she learned that the abortions may have played a role in the surgery she later had that was supposed to have left her unable to conceive. She was surprised to learn she was pregnant, but because Carlton was a childhood friend, she thought he'd be loving and supportive.

Carlton, on the other hand, could not have felt more trapped. After learning of her pregnancy, he immediately saw Karrie as manipulative and calculating. He was convinced that Karrie knew she could get pregnant and had set him up. He told her he thought she should have an abortion.

Karrie knew she faced an uphill battle. She'd have to complete her toughest year of law school and deal with her pregnancy at the same time. Then she'd have to take the bar examination and look for a job shortly after the baby was born. She had no idea how she'd support the baby financially; she couldn't support herself, let alone another child. But law school did teach her enough to know she'd better get her own attorney and go after child support.

Karrie's struggle is proof of how difficult collecting child support can be. Here she was a few months short of having her law degree, and she was getting nowhere in collecting support from Carlton. Her lawyer told her that Carlton hadn't filed income taxes in years. He claimed all his money belonged to his corporation, and that his parents paid for his personal expenses. The lawyer said she couldn't garnishee corporate funds, only personal income.

Finally, after her lawyer put together a plan and a proposal for how much support Carlton should provide, Karrie had to square off with Carlton before a judge. The judge ordered Carlton to pay four hundred dollars a month in child support, but told Karrie that since she was a lawyer, she could afford to pay her own attorney's fees.

Today, Karrie lives in a major U.S. city on forty-two-thousand dollars a year. She has yet to receive a child support check. After paying living expenses, daycare bills, and all the payments toward her maxed-out credit cards and her law school loans, she has hardly anything left to live on. She and her child live in a one-bedroom apartment. Fortunately, her baby's only two years old and Karrie's just beginning her career as an attorney. She's decided, once she gets over this hump, that she'll specialize in helping women collect child support.

Marie and T. J.

By the time I'd moved to the Tampa Bay area, my friend Marie, who lived in California, had given birth to a little girl. Marie called me

---

Keeping the Money Thing Separate

* Make a list of your feelings.

* Make a separate list of your children's needs.

* Whenever your emotions get the best of you, review the "needs" list.

* Get a lawyer or an advocate at the county attorney's office.

* Don't get emotional when you're before a judge or arbitrator.

* Don't blame your children's daddy in their presence for your money woes.

---

frequently to ask questions about breast-feeding, diapers, and daddies, and she was having a hard time with the daddy part of single mamahood.

T. J. wanted a relationship with his child, but before he invested his time and money, he wanted to be sure the baby was his. This infuriated Marie, because she had no doubts. The test proved what Marie knew all along—it was T. J.'s baby—and it also helped her lawyer get child support for Marie. By then, however, Marie's problem was compounded, for T. J. had gotten married, and his wife had a child of her own. At times, Marie felt rejected and hurt.

Marie had moved back to her hometown in Southern California, away from Los Angeles, where she'd met T. J., into her mother's condo, and started her own accounting business. Most of her big clients were still in L.A., so she had to travel there pretty regularly. That would make visitation a little easier, but child support would be a lot more complicated.

Once it was determined that T. J. was the baby's daddy, a court date was set where T. J. would be ordered to pay child support. But he'd challenged Marie's claims about the amount of money she was making as a self-employed CPA.

Marie did her work from an office at the condo. She could no longer spend money on designer suits and "fly" haircuts; the money wasn't there. She tightened her belt and waited out the child support. Her child was nearly a year old before the situation finally got resolved.

To help her case, Marie found that she had to learn a lot about child support law. It seemed every time she had a court date, T. J. would have a reason to hold things up. It was almost as though he was testing her nerves in the hope that she would give up the fight.

Meantime, there were a lot of ugly scenes her daughter had to witness. Marie feared that she would lose her battle and become her daughter's only means of support, and she found herself drawing so close to her daughter that it was, at times, smothering for the child.

T. J. was always good about seeing his daughter. He made sure he was there to pick her up on time; he insisted on including her in his new family's life, vacations and all. This also frightened Marie. She argued that her daughter, who was not yet a year old, was far too young to be spending that much time away from her mother. Besides, Marie was nursing her. But Marie's lawyer told her that withholding visitation could be held against her in child support proceedings, so during the weekends that her baby daughter was away, Marie would pump extra milk to make sure T. J. had bottles of mother's milk and frozen sacks of it to defrost throughout the weekends. T. J. would be with his daughter. This also kept Marie's milk flow normal.

Finally, Marie started receiving child support, garnisheed from T. J.'s wages. But even then, she often felt possessive about her daughter and demonstrated hostility toward T. J.

I believe this story is a good example of how money becomes the symbol for many underlying issues that single mamas need to confront. We argue about money because it is the most pressing need and the most evident problem in many of our relationships. Often however, it is only a symptom of deeper issues, many of which are the very reasons why we were unable to make things work with our children's daddies in the first place.

Judy and Jake

Judy and Jake met in college. Popular and handsome, Jake was a fraternity boy. He made good grades, he was active in student government, and he was a ladies' man.

Judy was studious. Baby doll-cute, she stood just under five-feet and dressed like a fashion model. She always made good grades and she was fairly popular, but because of her height and her slight frame, she never felt that she was as much a woman as her girlfriends. When she met Jake, she couldn't believe he was really interested in her.

As time passed, Judy and Jake grew closer. Jake had graduated, but he was still dating Judy, and in her junior year, she got pregnant. After a few months, they married, but Judy never really felt the marriage was based on her husband's love for her. She always suspected it was because of the baby.

They named the baby Jake Jr. Things were rocky from the start and continued so throughout the marriage. Judy and Jake disagreed a lot and frequently yelled and cursed at one another. When Jake Jr. was three years old, the couple split up. Judy moved from Jacksonville, Florida, where the couple had gone to college and made their home, to Orlando.

To a large extent, Judy had gone on with her life, but she had still not resolved the issues of child support and visitation with Jake. He had been sending checks to Judy when he could, and he was in the habit of picking up his son on most weekends.

Judy began dating a lawyer pretty regularly. He told Judy she should be collecting regular child support and that she needed to get her divorce taken care of. Unfortunately her new boyfriend also acted as her attorney in trying to resolve the questions of financial support and visitation. When Jake learned that Judy's lawyer and her new boyfriend were the same person, he became furious. Instead of driving to Orlando to see his son, he started showing up at Judy's house for a series of angry confrontations. Then he stopped showing up at all.

Soon Judy stopped dating the lawyer. She was so exhausted by what she'd been through in trying to collect child support from Jake that she gave up the fight altogether. She also decided it was not really worth her while to try to get him to start seeing his son again. She just let it slide.

Then Judy got a job in Miami, and she started dating a guy named Danny. Things were going incredibly well, and fast. For the first time, she felt she had the kind of respect she needed. Plus, Danny liked Jake Jr. a lot. Judy was certain that Danny would make a terrific stepfather.

Within five months, Danny proposed, and Judy accepted. By now, she knew she wouldn't have to deal with Jake again.

Jake Jr. would ask about his dad sometimes, but Judy gave him vague answers; she wasn't sure how to handle it. She was concerned about disturbing the family balance—she and Danny were expecting a child, and they'd learned it would be a girl.

Jake Jr. was an exemplary child. He made good grades, stayed out of trouble, and was placed in gifted classes. He and Danny had a great relationship, and Jake Jr. got along well with his little sister, Crystal.

He applied to all the good colleges and was accepted at Purdue, where Danny had finished college. He went to the high school prom, grad night, and all the other fun activities that make senior year so memorable.

But as graduation approached, Jake Jr. could no longer hold in what he'd wanted to share with his mother for so many years. He sometimes missed his dad and wondered what his life would have been like had he formed a relationship with him. Judy told Jake Jr. that his father was in Jacksonville and that she didn't know why Jake hadn't contacted his son over the years. Nor could she explain satisfactorily why she hadn't tried to make the contact on her own.

When Judy told me this, I asked her why she hadn't made the attempt. She told me she had been afraid how Jake would react. She feared that after fifteen years, he would still be angry. They had never worked through the child support issue.

When I explained my theory about how fathers can feel guilty if they haven't paid support, it made sense to Judy, a lot of sense. She said she could see Jake having that problem, but she had still been afraid to contact him.

Stepfathers Are No Substitute for Support From Daddy

With or without a new man in your life, do what you can to ensure your children's father pays child support. This way, you won't have to feel guilty about your new man taking on a responsibility that really isn't his. Nor will you have to feel your children owe him unreasonable allegiance. At the same time, your children's father will have a reason to stay on the scene, in your children's lives. Often single mamas look at the new man as a way to be rescued from having to deal with the ex. But as long as your children's father is alive and breathing, with few exceptions (see Exceptions to the Rules chapter) he deserves to be in your children's lives, and they deserve to have his love.

Jake Jr. will go to college in the fall. So far, his parents have not called one another. If and when Jake Jr. ever sees his natural father again, it will probably be because of his own efforts.

13

Grandmothers

Grandmothers can be our best friends and our most feared foes. We need them, but they sure can be a pain. Often grandmothers have a hard time coping with the fact that their daughters are single mamas; when our boyfriends or husbands leave or die, our mothers are devastated. They hate seeing us go it alone, because most mothers dream the Cinderella dream for their daughters. They hope we'll be wise enough to spot and hold on to a man who will love us till the day we die. And he'd better have a good job. If we're widowed, they want our husbands replaced as soon as possible with someone better and richer than the one we lost. If the baby's daddy was a loser, they want him replaced with a winner, right away. Please excuse the generalizations, but grandmothers' behaviors are sometimes contrary to the teachings of healthy single mamahood, so we must learn to either ignore our mothers when they start trippin', or we must patiently school them in the art of single mamahood.

Before we can be successful in changing the way some of our mothers look at single mamahood, we must understand why they feel the way they do. We have to understand that our mothers were conditioned to believe that a woman's success is determined by the size of her husband's paycheck. When a woman has no man, there's no way (in our mothers' minds) to tell whether she's made it.

Somehow, this woman without her husband's paycheck throws all of our mothers' beliefs out of whack. It's confusing. Therefore, even if we are successful in our own right, we're never complete. This leaves our children's grandmothers feeling embarrassed and even guilty that we have not become the married women they always dreamed we'd become.

Grandmothers will subconsciously take out their pity and shame for their single-mama daughters on the grandchildren. They may make you feel terribly guilty when you ask them to babysit for a while, but as soon as you say, "okay, forget it, Mom, I'll handle it," they'll jump right in with, "I'm not saying I don't want to keep the kids, I'm just saying you need to be better about keeping them on a regular schedule," or: "Just don't make this a habit." You know the drill.

The mothers of single mamas have a way of making us feel we haven't the slightest idea of how to bring up kids. Don't let us try something our mothers never tried. I've seen single mothers ridiculed for using time-out to punish their children or for feeding them homemade baby food or for breast-feeding. At the same time, single mamas are reprimanded by their mothers for yelling at their children or, God forbid, for giving them a backhand.

One time, when my son was not quite two years old and we were at my mother's house, I popped him on the backside for something he did wrong. I wish I could remember what he did, but I know it must have been dangerous, because I can count on one and a half hands the number of times I've hit my kid. I could not believe my mother's reaction. She socked her twenty-seven-year-old single-mama daughter on the arm, and said, "Don't you ever hit him!" I swear she did.

I've talked to many grandmothers since becoming a single mama about this kind of craziness. At first they deny any deliberate attempts to make their daughters feel bad about being single mamas. Eventually they do admit taking out their anger on their daughters in passive-aggressive ways. The root of the problem is that many mothers of single mamas were at one time in their lives single mamas themselves, or they came close.

Once, while visiting Oklahoma City, my birthplace, with my infant son, I sat down and had a heart-to-heart talk with my mother's sister, whom I hadn't known well until then because I had grown up in California. I was surprised—no, shocked—to learn that my mother was pregnant with my oldest sister when she and my father married. I could not believe what I was hearing. How could I, with my inquiring mind, never have known that before? Surely this had to play at least a partial role in why my mother reacted to my single mamahood the way she did.

Back in the old days, mothers were not as open about their mistakes, misdeeds, and misgivings as we are today. Our mothers held (and still hold) a lot in. What we must understand is that our mothers had a lot more to cope with than we do. Not only did they have to raise their children and keep them from harm, they had to do it in a far more racist culture than most of us have ever been exposed to. They had to be strong in ways we cannot imagine. They never had the opportunity to go to a counselor to discuss their problems, or to go to a district attorney's office to get action on collecting child support, or even to talk to many people in or out of their families about their problems. Problems were a way of life. As a result, our mothers are not as skilled as we are in putting their secrets out on the table and dealing with them.

In many ways, our mothers are trapped, imprisoned by hardships of a long time ago. We must understand that behind their complaints to us about our poor parenting skills are fears they cannot express.

I submit to you, however, that if you persevere and if you're a proud single mama who puts her children first, you will show your mother that single mamahood is not a death sentence for a mother and her children. She will come to admire, perhaps even envy your closeness with your children. She will come to understand that you may just be better off without a man in your life and in your children's lives, at least until the right man comes along. She'll learn to respect your ability to cope with your child's problems. By doing the single-mamahood thing correctly, you'll win over your own mother in ways you'll never imagine.

At first, your mother will think you're crazy to want to maintain a friendly relationship with your children's father. She'll believe, no matter how much you protest, that you're just trying to get him back. After all, that's what women used to do all the time. She will not understand how you can be on speaking terms with his new girlfriend and new wife. From time to time, she'll remind you that it's not necessary for you to reveal to this woman any of your "business."

When your mother gets on this kind of roll, you just have to ignore her. Don't get into an argument with her. Simply understand that she loves you and she's doing the best she can with the tools she has to work with and the hand she was dealt when she was young.

When Grandma's the Full-Time Parent

When a single mama dumps her responsibilities (including children) on her mother, other problems can develop. There are some single mamas who take advantage of their mothers, often when the grandmas are elderly. I'm not saying a grandma shouldn't be actively involved in the lives of her grandchildren if that is what she wants, I'm just saying that you need to be considerate. You're the one who had the child, and you're the one your child wants as a mother.

I've seen single mothers get an attitude when their mothers are unwilling to care for the grandchildren—but stop to think how unfair it is to impose your responsibility on your mother. She's already spent her entire adult life taking care of you and your brothers and sisters. Why do you expect her to take care of your kid, too?

Too often, grandparents are full-time parents of single-mama children. They're the ones who enroll the kids in school, take them to the doctor's office, and show up at their football games. Meantime, the real mama never experiences what real parenting, real responsibility is about. And guess who suffers? The children.

Sometimes kids get so used to the love they get from their grandmas and don't experience with their own single mamas, that they come to prefer it. They tell themselves that Grandma's the one who's raising them, and they convince themselves that that's okay. I'm sure with many children of single mamas, it *is* okay. But many of my adult friends have told me that they resented that their single mamas weren't there for them more.

Schooling Grandma

* Tell her you love her, but that you'd like to make some mistakes on your own.
* Tell her you appreciate her advice, but not necessarily the way she gives it.
* Make your need clear.
* Realize that she adds an important element to your children's lives.
* Remind her that she's special to you and the kids.
* Tell her "Thank you" on a regular basis.
* Don't argue with her in front of the kids.
* Tell her your feelings about single mamahood and ask her to read this book, or at least this chapter.

Jewel Ann

It took my mother, Jewel Ann, a long time to get used to the idea that I was a mother, let alone a single mama. The ironic thing is that my son, Winston, looks just like her; he could be her son. So she couldn't help falling in love with him at first sight.

Before I tell you about my relationship with my mother since I've become a single mama, you should understand what it was like before. I absolutely adore my mother—always have and always will. She is the most beautiful woman in the world, and the wisest, too. My mother, who tells everyone to call her Jewel, was raised in Okmulgee, Oklahoma, with her fifteen brothers and sisters. I was told there was one more, a twin, who died in childbirth or shortly thereafter. My mother's parents were sharecroppers, so she did her share of picking cotton, too.

My mother's first move off the farm was to Oklahoma City. She went to Mercy Hospital's nursing school and became a registered nurse. She eventually moved to California, but not before marrying and having three children. Kerry, my youngest sister, was born in Berkeley, California.

Jewel's first marriage was not a good one for her. But she was a Catholic girl who stuck it out as long as she could. By the time she and my father divorced, my eldest sister, Kim, was eleven. A couple of years later, she married Leon, the man of most women's dreams. He brought his three boys and an incredible amount of stability and security to our family.

My mother first met Winston when he was just a month old. She and Leon flew from California to New York to check him out. When Teddy and I met her at the airport, Winston was tucked away in my Snuggly, looking like a little turtle. As soon as she spotted us in the airport, she lit up. I saw a look on her face I'd never seen before. When I unzipped the pouch, Winston's eyes opened, and I saw tears well up in my mother's eyes. When she looked at Winston's face, she saw her own eyes. She could hardly hold back the excitement. From that moment on, my mother was in love with Winston.

At first, I saw my mother's reminders about diapers and baby food as just grandma stuff; I wasn't threatened at all. Besides, I was nursing Winston, and my mother never nursed any of her babies. So there was only so much she could tell me. It wasn't until later, when Winston was a year old, and we'd moved to Los Angeles, that I started to resent her advice.

When we first moved to California, my mother would remind me that she'd welcome visits from Winston as long as Teddy or I came along. In other words, she was not going to become one of those grandmas who provides full-time care for her grands. This bothered me, because quite frankly, I'd never asked her to be a full-time parent for my kid.

During our visits, she'd constantly interfere with my parenting. "What are you feeding him, Kelly?" "Kelly, can't you tell he's tired? Put him to bed." "How many times have you changed him?" I couldn't believe it. I wondered what she thought I did when she wasn't there.

I asked Leon about it, but the problem is, Leon supports his wife one hundred percent, no matter what she does. He said he knew it bothered me but that I should look at it as my mom's attempt to

How My Mother and I Worked It Out

* Respected one another's opinions
* Checked our egos
* Kept our distance
* Did not use my son as a pawn
* Practiced patience

help me out. "She's not trying to hurt your feelings, Kelly. She's just trying to help, that's all. I don't think she doesn't think you know what you're doing."

Finally, I had to sit down with my mother and let her know how I felt. "I feel inadequate when you tell me how to take care of Winston," I told her. "I feel hurt when you imply that I'm being irresponsible," etc. She would apologize, but her overbearing ways pretty much continued until Winston was nearly four, when he and I moved from California to Florida.

I don't see my mother that much anymore, perhaps just once a year, so it's no longer a problem. In fact, over the years, my mother has expressed her pride in my ability to raise my son on my own. She tells me I'm a great mother and that I've done a terrific job with Winston. Of course, there were times when she'd tell me she just knew I'd find someone special. Once, when I was buying my first house, she told me I was putting myself under too much pressure. "Why don't you wait till you remarry before you buy a house?" she said. She could not understand how I could plan my life out without the hope and dream of a man joining me.

Even though my mother now realizes that, by the grace of God, I'm doing okay, I think she feels sorry for me because I'm a single mama. She's not a convert to this whole single-mamahood thing yet, but I believe she's coming around.

Cornelius

Cornelius was always with one of his uncles—Bobby and Stan were more like big brothers than uncles—and Stan was his favorite. They even looked alike. Both were tall for their age and lanky with thick hair, which in the late seventies meant it had to be braided regularly in order to comb out easily into an afro. Uncle Bobby was two years older than Stan.

Cornelius lived with his grandmother and grandfather and two uncles from the time he was three. His mother was a model, working in Europe most of the time. Cornelius thought she was the most beautiful woman he'd ever seen, and he was proud to have her as his mother.

"Corn," as his uncles nicknamed him, always expected his mother to come to get him from Grandma's house to live with her again. In fact, she told him the stay would only be temporary. But it seemed with every change his mama made, whether it be a job or a man, she couldn't find a place in her life for Corn.

I met Corn when he was four. I was fifteen at the time and had a crush on his Uncle Stan. Stan, on the other hand, saw me as merely a friend, whom he could rely on to babysit Corn for free while he was running the streets.

In a way, Corn became a part of our family for a while. We all thought he was cute and sweet. Corn grew really close to me, and, in retrospect, I think it had a lot to do with his absentee mama. I would help him with his homework, play card games with him, ride bikes, whatever. On many weekends, I'd go over to Stan's house just to hang out with Corn. He would get all excited when he saw me, and I'm a sucker for a kid who's crazy about me.

I started spending a lot of time with Corn's grandma, too. She told me she could tell how much her little grandson missed his mama. Without putting her daughter down too much, she would tell me she wished Corn's mama would find a place to settle down, that Corn could be there. Sometimes, when Corn and Bobby and Stan were working on her nerves all at the same time, I'd wonder whether it was fair that she should have to raise her grandson.

Corn's grandma told me her daughter was only sixteen when she had Corn, and that she didn't have any business having a baby. I sensed that she felt guilty for not keeping a tighter rein on her daughter. Grandmas who end up raising their single-mama daughters' kids often do it out of guilt. That's not to say they don't love

When Grandma's the Primary Parent

* If your kids must live with Grandma, make it temporary, while you're working on an educational goal or a work assignment.
* Do not make promises to your kids that you can't keep.
* Do not take advantage of your mother. Instead, put yourself in her shoes.
* Help your parents with financial support. Put them on a child support schedule.
* Remember, they're your kids, not your parents'.

their grandchildren, but many of them would much rather be doing something else.

Corn grew up to be a well-rounded young man. He's in college now. But his mama never did come back to get him, as she promised. There's no telling what long-term affect that important empty promise will have on Corn's life.

14

Peace, Love, and Spirituality

Your children's peace is the key to your happiness as a single mama. Children are most secure when they know what to expect, when there is discipline in their lives and moral leadership in their homes. How family members treat one another is crucial in their early years. The more peace they see, the better. Peace will foster a sense of calm in their lives. Peace will offer normalcy, and make family their refuge from all the challenges they face at school and in their everyday lives.

Childhood is a time to explore, to enjoy, to experiment. It's a time to stumble, to hurt, and to make mistakes. Through the roller coaster of childhood, kids need a comfort zone; they need a place that makes sense when nothing else does; they need a place to call home. For kids of single mamas, that place is not necessarily where they put their heads down at night. It is a place in their hearts where they feel loved and supported. It is a place that makes them feel secure. Sometimes it may be mama's house; other times, it's daddy's house or Grandma's or Auntie Kim's or Uncle Billy's. Nothing creates turmoil in that place in their hearts more than friction. It is imperative that you do everything in your power to respect and honor your children's comfort zone. Already, a lot is asked of your children. They must accept the fact that their household is headed by a single woman. They must accept that they cannot see Daddy when they want to. They must make compromises because of a choice that was not theirs. The least you can do for them is make their comfort zone a peaceful place.

In many ways, the peace you give your children will make up for some things you're unable to give them as a single mama. I have seen single mamas give their children every material possession in the world, and yet the kids are never satisfied. They take and take and demand more. They know their mamas are trying to give them "things" to make up for the intangible thing they need most. Some are single mamas who refuse to humble themselves enough to indulge an ex's mother or sister's wish to spend time with their child. Some single mamas fight with their own mothers in front of their children. Some single mamas are so concerned with their pride that they refuse to see that their artificial affection is transparent.

Forgiving

Some people hold on to resentment for their entire lives. But as a single mama, your inability to forgive and move on will have an impact on your life as well as your children's. I remember I used to think I could hate Teddy and still function as a whole, complete woman, but I was so wrong. It took church for me to figure it out.

Spirituality is extremely important for successful single mamahood. Religion will help your children learn to put life's good and bad aspects in perspective, and they will grow to understand the importance of order. More important, a spiritually guided household fosters love and understanding in the family.

One day, in Sunday school, I came across a biblical text that changed the way I felt about Teddy. It actually allowed me to forgive him and move on with my life: "Anyone who claims to be in the light but hates his brother is still in the darkness. Whoever loves his brother lives in the light, and there is nothing in him to make him stumble. But whoever hates his brother is in the darkness and walks around in the darkness; he does not know where he is going, because the darkness has blinded him." (I John 9:11)

I thought about how Jesus constantly forgives me for all the stupid and hurtful things I do and all the things I've done in the past.

Someone in the class made reference to the Book of Luke: "But I tell you who hear me; Love your enemies, do good to those who hate you, bless those who curse you, pray for those who mistreat you. If someone strikes you on one cheek, turn to him the other also. If someone takes your cloak, do not stop him from taking your tunic. Give to everyone who asks you, and if anyone takes what belongs to you, do not demand it back. Do to others as you would have them do to you." (Luke 7:27-31)

There was more: "Do not judge, and you will not be judged. Do not condemn, and you will not be condemned. Forgive, and you will be forgiven." (Luke 7:37)

I read these passages over and over again. And I made up my mind: I would free myself of all the hatred I had for Teddy. I would forgive him and move on with my life. Oh happy day!

Freedom and Happiness

Once your children sense your freedom, they'll respond positively. Do not expect your children not to hold grudges at school and to get along with the kids in the neighborhood if you can't get along with your family and your children's family. Do what you can to make your relationship with your ex and his family work.

Let's say your children's father is irresponsible. He makes a habit of promising your children he'll take them to a special place or buy them a special toy, and he never comes through. Then one day he keeps a promise to take the kids to a movie; he even shows up on time. Your response should not be, "It's about time. The kids say you never keep your promises. You're always disappointing them." Instead, it should be, "Hey, thanks. Little Joey is going to be so excited when I tell him you're here. He's been looking forward to this all day. I'm so glad you'll make it there early. Have fun." I know, I know. This is totally out of character for you, and the scoundrel doesn't deserve such good treatment. Besides, you couldn't possibly say all those gushy things to this man who cheated on you and lied to you for all those years. But just try it, and see what a difference it makes. Don't look for gratitude from your ex; don't even expect a thank you. Just watch your kids and see how they behave when they're near you and their father. They'll be so happy. Watch them smile, watch how they swing back and forth or how they say little nice things to you. It's because when you are free, so are they. The whole family is free and your children know they can fly like a bird in the sky.

So much of the strain and tension that exists after a couple goes its separate ways has to do with the couple's family members. People are so used to there being a lot of friction involved during breakups, especially when kids are involved, that they can sometimes create problems where none exist. When they see you getting along with your children's stepmother or their aunts and uncles on their father's side, they'll think you've lost your mind. Or they'll assume you're being taken advantage of. It seems many family members of single mamas would much rather see you fighting that getting along.

If you're planning special occasions for your children—a birthday party or a graduation or a piano recital—invite everyone. If some of those you invite have something negative to say about someone else you invited, even if the complainer is your sister, tell her she doesn't have to attend if she has a problem with it. Be nice, but be firm. Your attempts to bring together the people your children love is the correct one. Don't let other people's problems become your problems.

Sometimes single mamas will let the man they're dating dip into their business. Some men are so possessive, they'd rather see fighting between their girlfriend and her ex's family than to have peace and see everyone happy. Always consider this when a guy you're seeing starts creating problems between you and your child's paternal family. Remember, nine times out of ten, the family will be around longer than your guy. If you do end up marrying him, things could be real ugly, unless he decides to get over his anger. No single mama needs a bitter, jealous man in her life. Her children certainly don't need one either.

Choosing a Church

* Consider your family church first.
* Talk to other single mamas.
* Visit lots of churches until you find one you like.
* Make sure the church has age-appropriate programs and ministries.
* Look for a church with single-parent support groups.
* Ask whether "singles" programs are single-mama friendly.
* Look for a church with a firm spiritual and biblical foundation, so that it keeps you on track.

Evan

For as long as he could remember, Evan went to church. His mother would always get him there early enough to go to Sunday school.

For Evan, church was a place to play with his friends and to learn about God. In fact, it was in church where Evan first learned that divorce was bad.

"Mommy, why did you and Daddy get a divorce?"

"Evan, we just didn't love each other and we were doing things that hurt one another. We didn't want you to see us being mean all the time, and we didn't like it ourselves."

"In the Bible, it says you're not supposed to get a divorce, except for marital unfaithfulness. What is marital unfaithfulness anyway, Mama?"

"It's not treating one another fairly. It's breaking the special bond mommies and daddies are supposed to have."

Evan didn't ask any more questions. But as he grew into his teen years, he pretty much figured it out. He wasn't sure who had cheated on whom, but he did know that he would never be unfaithful to his wife. He also knew that his child would be raised in his home with the child's mother.

Church taught Evan a lot about values. It also exposed him to the kind of men he wished his dad was. His father didn't spend much time with him, but the church had a lot of mentoring programs that he took part in. He got to go to work with his mentor, and he spent lots of time hanging out with him and his family. Evan was determined to be like the men in the church.

15

Exceptions to the Rules

But what if none of the single-mamahood rules we have studied so far fits your life? What if your children's father is simply nowhere on the scene, or he's in jail, or he's just a plain loser? What then?

Believe it or not, there's an answer. Many single mamas have no choice but to keep their children's fathers out of their lives. Clearly these mamas have to live by their own set of rules.

My first bit of advice to you mamas is to get involved with support groups for widows, or with wives of inmates, or with other narrow-focus groups for single mamas. If a local support group does not exist that fits your situation, form your own. Put up notices on bulletin boards at your church, college, apartment complex, or neighborhood center. Find women like yourself so you know you're not alone. Only women who are walking in your shoes can provide exactly the kind of support you need.

When Daddy's Dead

Women whose husbands are deceased must proceed as though they are single with no husband. However, they must make sure their children know they had a father who loved and supported them and their mother. They must know their father did not choose to leave the earth, but that God called him home. Your children should know their father's family. They should hear stories about him, see videos and photos, and feel they have the right to speak freely of their father's love for them. If you decide to become involved with another man, continue to let your children make the choice about the degree to which they want to talk about their father. As they grow closer to other men in their lives, they'll probably choose to visit their father's photo albums and videos less frequently. However, never discourage this kind of reminiscing. Do not take away your children's right to love their father, even after he's gone.

When Daddy's in Jail

The latest statistics show that one in three young African-American men is in some way linked to the justice system. Many are in jail or prison. What if your children's father is one of them? First, you must be honest with your children. Do not tell them their father is on vacation or on a work-related trip; tell them the truth. If you don't, someone else will. Explain to your children that their father is not a bad person, but that he did a bad thing. Respond to each of their questions with a concise answer. Do not give them any more or less information than they're ready at their age to hear.

If your children's father is in jail, let them know you think it's okay for them to visit him. Tell them you think it's all right if they wish to continue to see their father and to share their lives with him, that you think it would make their lives complete. Your children may choose to stay away, but at least they'll know they have your blessing if they change their minds. And make sure you provide the transportation if your children are not of driving age.

Let your children know it's okay to write to their incarcerated father. The relationship obviously would be good for your ex, but it may also be good for your kids. The key is choice. Do not discourage your children from wanting to be involved with their daddy just because he's locked up.

Although recidivism is high in our nation's jails, the fact is many men eventually do get out of jail, and when they do, they may want to see their children. It is best that your children do not learn of

---

Single Mama's Role When Daddy's in Jail

✳ Tell your kids the truth.

✳ Allow them to write to Daddy.

✳ Do not discourage visits.

✳ Do not force children to write or visit if they are uncomfortable with it.

---

their father's existence the day he is released from jail. We may think we're protecting our kids by keeping information from them, but the truth is very different. Talk to some of your adult friends about shocking information they learned as older children or adults. They'll tell you they would have preferred to know the truth early. Kids of single mamas have enough dysfunction to deal with. Your job is to do whatever you can to keep it to a minimum.

When Daddy's Unavailable

There are other times when your children's father falls off the face of the earth. He may have a serious drug problem, be involved with a cult, or be deep into some sort of illegal activity. If you got pregnant on a one-night stand or after knowing your child's father for a few months, you may have learned during your pregnancy that he is not the type of man who should be around kids. He could even have a record that includes a murder, rape, child abuse, or child sex abuse conviction. Exposing your child to such a man could be a tragedy. It is both your right and your obligation to keep your child away from his or her father in most of these cases.

So what do you do in cases like this when your children ask about Daddy? Again, the truth is the best policy. If your kid is three years old the truth does not have to be, "Your daddy's a child molester." It could be the truth as a three-year-old understands it. "Honey, you know how you have to go to time-out if you misbehave?

Well if grownups misbehave, they get punished, too. Sometimes their behavior is so bad they have to go to jail, or they have to stay away from people who they might hurt. Your daddy hurt a child. That's why your daddy's not here."

Of course, as the children mature, your answer can become more sophisticated. Whatever you do, do not keep the truth a mystery. As I said before, eventually it will surface. You should be the one controlling how the story unfolds.

Whatever you do, do not tell your child that his or her father is bad. Just say he did something that is wrong or bad. If you tell the kid his daddy is a bad man, he may see himself as a bad child. After all, isn't your child a product of this man? If you keep the negative description only to the behavior, your child will understand that people make choices about what to do with their lives.

How you choose to handle the relatives of your child's father, if you've decided to keep him out of your life, depends on the circumstances and the family. I wouldn't push my child on the family. However, if people in the family are trustworthy and wish to see your child, consider it. Make sure you know them and trust them, however, before you allow unsupervised visits. You may want to include the paternal grandparents or aunts and uncles at your family activities or your child's birthday parties. But be careful. Always keep your eyes on your child. Trust needs to be earned, not given freely, especially when it involves your children.

When You're the Adoptive Single Mama

Another exception I have not discussed heretofore is adoption. Sometimes single women become single mamas by virtue of having adopted a child. Many states allow single women to adopt kids, especially the so-called hard-to-place kids—in other words African-American and biracial babies and children with special physical and emotional needs. Clearly the father factor is nonexistent in most of these cases. Unless you adopted a child in one of those scenarios where you know the daddy, and he consented to the adoption because he accepts that he's unable to care for his child, your child

---

Get a Safe Deposit Box

If you have any photos of, or documents about your child's father, keep them, and if possible, make photocopies. It would be wise to keep the originals in a bank safe deposit box. That way, if there's ever a fire or an accident, you won't lose the only connection your children have to their daddy.

---

really has no father. Here, again, you must be truthful in handling any and all daddy questions. You'll have to tell your child he or she is adopted. When your kid's at an age where he or she understands, you'll have to explain exactly what the adoption entailed. Whatever you do, do not try to "male mend" your situation. Do not size up every man you date, looking for a father for your child. If you're waiting for this kind of rescue, you're probably setting yourself up for a hard fall. Few men decide to be with you because they are dying to raise your child, let alone someone else's. Your chances of meeting someone who's going to be an "ideal" father to your adopted child are as slim as they are if your child is your own. I'm not saying it never happens; just don't count on it, or your life may be disappointing, and you certainly won't be focusing on what's really important—successful single mamahood.

In the case of the adoptive child, if you're fortunate enough to have photographs of the biological father or mother, save them. Make a special scrapbook for your child. Let him know that whenever he needs to look at the photos, you'll make them available. Keep the scrapbook in a safe place, away from the child, however. You don't want to make it too accessible. Remember that when kids have a bad day and become angry, they often take out their frustrations on the people they love. You'll get over it if they say something nasty to you, but once a photo's torn up into tiny pieces, there's no putting it back together again.

Make sure in these special circumstances, where there's an exception to the rule, that your child's life is full of love.

Grandparents, uncles, aunts, cousins—all these folks should be in your children's lives. No matter what, your children should feel loved.

Sarah and Tito

Sarah met Tito in a bowling league. Friends of hers, a married couple, made the introduction. He was about six-foot-three, and since Sarah was six feet tall, she felt an immediate attraction. For whatever reasons, people were always trying to hook her up with short men; to Sarah, that included just about every guy in Long Beach.

Sarah and Tito hit it off. He didn't try to impress her by telling her he had a whole lot of money. Overstating who they are is one of Sarah's pet peeves about men. Tito was athletic; he liked talking about sports and politics—two subjects Sarah enjoyed. Best of all, he wasn't from Long Beach. It seemed all the Long Beach men were past tired.

After dating Tito for about three months, Sarah knew she was in love, and Tito told her he was in love with her. Not only that, he bought her a ring. They didn't hesitate to set a wedding date, nor did they hesitate to get married. One weekend, four months after they met, Tito and Sarah eloped.

A month later, Sarah was pregnant, and she was already experiencing "buyer's remorse" about Tito. He was always broke, and she started catching him in little lies. Still, she was excited about the prospect of being a mother.

One afternoon, Tito, who did not have a car of his own, borrowed Sarah's car to run errands. About an hour after he left the house, Sarah got a phone call from her cousin, Kendra.

"Sarah," Kendra said, nearly hyperventilating. "You won't believe what I just heard."

"What?" Sarah asked anxiously.

"My friend Brenda and I are at the park in the car having lunch. We've been here about forty-five minutes. A few minutes ago, we saw Tito in your Jeep. We both said at the same moment, 'There goes my cousin's husband.' Girl—Tito is married to another woman."

What Sarah Did Right

❊ Distanced herself from her child's daddy
❊ Told her child the truth
❊ Kept photos to share with her child
❊ Made it possible for her child to have a good relationship with Granddaddy

---

Sarah had to sit down. She was both humiliated and furious.

"Thank you," she said. "He's driving up now."

Sarah confronted Tito, and he admitted it to her. Not only that, he took off in her Jeep. When she called the police to report the vehicle stolen, they told her she couldn't—that if her husband had her car, it wasn't stolen.

A few days later, Tito returned the Jeep. By then, Sarah had gotten his other wife's phone number. After hearing the bigamous tale, she sent Sarah a copy of their marriage certificate so that Sarah could start annulment proceedings. Sarah had already packed all of Tito's things. She told him where to collect them (at his sister's house), and said that she never wanted to see him again.

After Sarah's daughter, Bree, was born, she received a call from Tito's sister, who told her that Tito had left some baby clothes at her house for Sarah to pick up. But Sarah chose not to. She had subsequently learned that Tito had four children with his other wife. She made up her mind never to accept a thing from this man, and not to look at him as the father of her daughter.

Bree is four years old now. She has asked about her father only once.

"Do I have a daddy?" she asked. "Yes you do." "Where is he?" "I'll show you," Sarah answered. She went to her bedroom and pulled a snapshot out of a dresser drawer. "Here he is." Bree hasn't enquired about her father since.

Sarah's decided that whenever her daughter asks about her dad, she'll answer the specific question. She doesn't want to lie about him, realizing that wouldn't be fair to her daughter.

Sarah hopes to marry sometime in the future, because she'd like Bree's stepfather to become the man whom she considers her dad. I gave her the speech about living in the present, accepting her circumstances the way they are so that her daughter does not think her family is not complete without some man, any man. Sarah says she understands. I just hope she finds the right man, since it's clear to me she hasn't totally subscribed to the Gospel According to Single Mamahood.

Fortunately, Sarah does involve her child in her parents' lives, especially her dad's. She wants Bree to at least know how a daddy's supposed to behave.

Little Leon and Tracy

Tracy told me she can hardly remember a time when her son, Leon, was not sick. He was diagnosed with leukemia before his first birthday, and from that time on went in and out of remission. Tracy didn't have much of a career, and tended to go from one job to another. Because of Leon's illness, however, keeping a job was hard.

Leon would sometimes spend months at a time in the hospital. He'd go through periods where he was on the brink of death and then, he would bounce back and be in remission for a while. By the time Leon turned four, doctors told Tracy his only hope for a normal life would be to receive bone marrow transplant.

Leon's exposure to doctors, nurses, and hospital-speak made him quite precocious. He was mannish, but also charming and sweet. He always wore a huge smile and a great attitude. Tracy had no idea how long she would have her son, so she rarely left his side.

I first met Leon at my church; he was the guest of one of the member families. Winston and I noticed him about the same time, made eye contact with him, and played quietly with him, the way you do with stranger kids at church. After services, he came over to our pew and talked to us. It was hard to believe this child was only four. He spoke as if he were a wise old man. He asked us whether he'd see us again, and he suggested I give his mother a call. He even gave me the telephone number.

During service that day, when the minister came to the part when people do prayer requests, someone requested a special prayer for Leon. They said he was a little boy who needed a bone marrow transplant. I remembered hearing about the boy on the radio. After the service when Leon spoke to us I asked him about the bone marrow transplant, and he gave me lots of information, far more than you'd expect from a four-year-old—even from a four-teen-year-old.

Later, I called Leon's mom. We got to know each other very well, and she shared her story with me for my health segment on television. After I got to know Tracy better, she told me that she had conceived Leon when she was very young; she hadn't even finished high school. She told me that Leon knew the whole story of why he didn't know his father. She was a real single mama, one who lived by all the principles described in this book. Although she did not know where Leon's father was and had no pictures of him, she described him as best she could to Leon when he asked. She was 100 percent involved in Leon's life—she'd visited his teachers and made sure he had appropriate role models. Tracy was an amazing mama, who somehow knew naturally how to do it right.

Meantime, Tracy's sisters and mother gave her a hard time. They were always telling her that Leon was the one running the show, and that he needed to be disciplined better. They disapproved of her parenting style, and they seemed to have no clue what Tracy was going through day in and day out, not knowing whether Leon was going to live or die. Still, despite her feelings about her family, Tracy made sure Leon spent as much time with them as he could. Basically, she put up with her sisters' and mother's belittling and berating for the sake of Leon, who needed their love. She realized she could not convert them to her way of thinking, nor could she convince them that she knew what she was doing. But that was her problem, not Leon's.

Through Leon, Tracy seemed to find her calling. She became active in the city's bone marrow recruitment efforts. She began giving speeches in public forums, encouraging people to join the national marrow program. She also joined a church; that did a lot for Leon, too.

Tracy was tested to see if her marrow was a good match for her son's, but unfortunately it wasn't. Her doctor then asked her about Leon's dad. Tracy had to admit that she had no idea where he was. Tracy told me she had gone to a party one night, had gotten drunk and had allowed a man she met there to have sex with her. She remembered what he looked like, but couldn't recall his name; ever since that night, she had tried to forget the incident had ever occurred. Nine months later, after Leon was born, she had started her own little investigation to try to find Leon's dad, but he'd never come forward. She got to the point where she was 80 percent sure who the man was. When she approached him, however, he acted as if he'd never seen her in his life. It was a case where knowing Leon's father could have been more important than helping her son to be happy and secure. The father's bone marrow might possibly save his life.

So Tracy bent all her energies to finding a donor for Leon. She appeared on television and radio, pleading for people to get tested to see if they were a match for her son. But all the recruiting never paid off for Leon. Even with a perfect bone marrow match, a child's chances of surviving are still about fifty-fifty, at best. Unfortunately Tracy's own marrow matched only three of the six genetic factors present in her son's marrow. But doctors had decided that if Leon's white blood cell counts fell so low that his life was in danger, they'd try an experimental procedure where they manipulate a family member's marrow to make it more similar to the recipient's marrow.

At first it seemed to work. Leon lived well past the first four weeks when rejection typically occurs. He even went home and, in some ways, returned to a relatively normal life. But two months later, it happened—rejection. At age twenty-two, Tracy lost her baby.

I went to the funeral, and it seemed as though a good portion of the city turned out. Children had drawn special cards for Leon; his friends sang his favorite songs. Nurses and community leaders shared stories of how this little boy touched their lives. Everyone talked about how special he was. They spoke of how he was a

What I Learned From Tracy

I learned that even when single mamahood is tough on me, there's always someone struggling with greater burdens. It is so important for single mamas to support one another, and most important, to not judge one another. It would be easy to blame Tracy for not knowing who her child's father was, but I've lived long enough to know that we all have our own mistakes and skeletons. I certainly have my own share of them.

Single mamas must be strong, stronger than other women. I don't know many married women or men who could have done what Tracy did. Today, she's looking for a job and doing everything she can to start all over again. With all she's been through and survived, there's no reason to think she won't be successful.

reflection of his wonderful, dedicated mother. Finally, even Tracy's family saw that she had given her son everything a mother could give, and then some.

16

Healthy Single Mamahood

Single mamas are so busy taking care of their children that they often neglect themselves. In order to be a good single mama, however, you need to be healthy, which means you must get proper nutrition as well as plenty of rest and exercise. You also must see to it that your children maintain good health. All of this takes organization.

If you are pregnant, now's as good a time as any to get on the road to good health. Eat well-balanced, low-fat meals, and get plenty of exercise. A half-hour walk three times a week will work wonders for your body and your mind. Talk to your doctor before you make any drastic changes.

Healthy single mamahood requires that you spend time with each of your children, if possible every day. Taking walks in the evening with your children allows you to wind down with a quiet talk about your day and theirs. Then you can give the children a few minutes of your time before they go to bed, and read to the little ones after their baths.

Scheduling is very important to maintain good mental and physical health. That means you need to plan each stage of your day's beginning—moving the kids along from bed, to bathroom, to kitchen, preparing breakfast, getting yourself ready for the workday, and heading out the door. The routine will keep you from having to yell at the kids while you frantically try to pull loose ends together.

I've tried a lot of schedules, making adjustments when necessary, and I've found this one works well for me in the morning:

Get up at 6 A.M.
Work out until 7 A.M.; read paper on treadmill.
Make Winston's lunch at 7:05.
Wake Winston at 7:10.
Eat breakfast and talk till 7:30.
Get dressed and make sure Winston dresses till 8:30.
Get Winston to bus stop by 8:40.
Get to work by 9:00 A.M.

If your children are still too young to dress themselves, you might find dressing them before you get ready in the morning is more efficient than doing it after. That way, the little ones can color or watch something educational on TV while you get ready, and you won't have to worry about fighting with them about what they're going to wear when you need to be leaving the house.

Evenings can be crazier than mornings, since a lot of what happens depends on your work schedule. If you work a daytime schedule, you might try something like this:

Leave work.
Pick kids up from sitter's or daycare.
Check on homework (it should be done right after school).
Make dinner (using paper plates).
Clean up while kids pick out clothes for the following day.
Take walk.
Bathe little kids or supervise bathing for older kids.
Put younger kids to bed.
Let older kids have time to themselves for reading, playing, talking on telephone.
Put older kids to bed by 10 P.M..
Talk to friends on phone, read, or entertain guests.
Be in bed by 11 P.M., midnight at the latest.

When your children are playing sports or taking part in other after-school activities, you'll have to make adjustments to your schedule. You can exercise at the same park where your son is having football practice or take an aerobics class in the community center where your kids are taking karate or practicing for their dance recital or basketball game. Be flexible, but try to stick as closely as possible to your routine. The less hectic your life, the better you will relate to your children, and the better they'll do in school.

Low-Fat Fast Meals

A healthy single mama feeds her family and herself well-balanced, low-fat meals. She keeps fresh fruit in the house for snacks. Baby carrots, raw broccoli, and raw cauliflower also make good, nutritious snacks. There's a general belief that it takes a lot of time and energy to prepare healthy meals, but in fact the opposite is true. It takes a lot of time to prepare fattening meals, not healthy ones.

Here are a couple of my favorite quick dinners.

Fresh broiled fish, steamed vegetables, and rice   Simply broil your favorite fish cutlets in a flat baking dish. Steam any vegetables in a stove-top steamer. And cook rice in a stove-top pot. Total preparation time: twenty minutes.

Quesadillas, refried beans, tossed salad   Shred Cheddar cheese. Place a handful of cheese in flour tortillas, and fold over once. Microwave for 20 seconds. Season canned refried beans with salsa. Microwave in bowl for approximately thirty seconds. Cut up lettuce and tomatoes and mix in salad bowl. Total preparation time: three minutes.

Broiled chicken breasts, pasta and tomato sauce, steamed veggies or tossed salad   Marinate chicken in Italian salad dressing and steak sauce or barbecue sauce for about three minutes. Add seasonings to taste to ready-made spaghetti sauce and warm on stove. Boil pasta. Broil chicken breasts until done. Total preparation time: twenty-five minutes.

The more you cook, the more ideas you'll come up with. Share ideas with your single-mama friends, too. Since sometimes your older children may be home alone, allow them to prepare the microwaveable meals. Also keep on hand sandwich meats and bread so the kids can make sandwiches when you won't make it home for dinner. Winston likes microwaveable pizza, too. Keeping enough food in the house for dinner will save you lots of money that you won't have to spend on fast food and eating out.

Good Health Care

I've heard too many excuses from single mamas about why they don't go to the doctor when they're sick or why they put off health screenings that every woman should have routinely. But there is no excuse for not maintaining your health. If you are sick, go to the doctor. If you feel you're going crazy, you probably are, so see a counselor, a psychologist, or a psychiatrist.

Have your teeth cleaned twice a year; your children's, too. Schedule their appointments during your lunch hour, or take a vacation day or sick day from work to take care of as many appointments as you can. See your gynecologist every year for a Pap smear and breast exam. If you're forty or have a history of breast cancer in your family, schedule annual mammograms, and no matter what your age is, do monthly breast self-exams.

17

Discipline

How many times have you threatened your children by saying they would have to go live with their daddy, as if it were a death sentence? I'm guilty as charged—but I know I'm wrong. There are much better ways for a single mama to discipline her children. First, keep in mind that the word *discipline* means to teach, to instruct, to guide, to nurture, to develop. Disciplining your children does not mean putting them down or kicking their behinds. I repeat: a single mama should not kick her kid's behind. There are better ways.

The father of one of my son's friends is a real man's man—an old-school disciplinarian who believes a boy cannot receive proper discipline from his mother. He's also very active in Boy Scouts, and, for a while, motivated me to get Winston involved. This man believes discipline is about having a large physical presence in a child's life. He believes in taking a belt to a boy's behind. He thinks this is something only a father can do.

I totally disagree with this form of discipline. To properly teach a child, I believe that you use the rod to guide him, not to beat him. My stepfather taught me that with the boys in my family. I never once saw him raise his hand to hit my brothers. When he saw that they were not paying attention to orders from him or that they were unruly in either way, he'd simply ask them if they were tired. Of

165

course, when they were little boys, they'd always answer, "No." Despite the answer, Leon would send them to bed. No yelling or screaming—just a simple, "time to go to bed." It must have worked, because all my brothers—and my sisters, too, for that matter— graduated college and made my parents proud.

Men who subscribe to the old-school form of discipline don't think single mamas are physically intimidating enough to beat their children into submission. I believe women who believe corporal punishment is the only way to discipline children will, in fact, have problems. But it has more to do with this discipline approach than with the mother's shortcomings in carrying it out.

Learning how to discipline your children is one of the best pieces of information you can take away from a single parenting class or support group. You'll learn how to talk to your children and to better understand the source of their frustrations and problems. You'll learn how to set parameters and rules, and how to take things away from your children that are really important to them, rather than taking out your frustration on them by whipping their behinds.

Discipline should always be age appropriate. Kids under two who act inappropriately—crying at the dinner table, throwing food, or spitting their pacifiers in your face—are simply being babies. They're communicating frustration or other bad feelings with you the only way they know. Remember, they cannot make words yet. Typically, when you have a problem like this, you've done something wrong. You've either gotten the baby off his schedule, or not changed him on time, or maybe you've taken him out to a fancy restaurant. Do not expect the infant to magically become an adult just because you put him in an adult world. Sometimes you'll get lucky, but eventually, your luck will wear thin.

Schedules, strictly adhered to, are the best thing in the world for babies. Once your baby's grown out of infancy—that is, once her cries at night are pleas for your comfort instead of for food—it's time to put her on a clock.

For me, putting a baby to bed about 8 P.M. is like magic. At first, your baby will cry a long time when you put him or her to bed at a certain time. This is especially true if the baby's used to going to bed with you. But after about three days, the baby will get it. And there will be peace in your home.

I have found that once a baby gets on an 8 P.M. bedtime schedule, he or she will sleep about twelve hours. Once you get the child up, immediately feed and clothe him. About five or six hours later, usually a little after lunch, your baby will probably start getting fussy. That means it's time for a nap. If you're traveling or you have company, keep your babies on schedule. You'll be amazed at what this does to improve their behavior. Babies who get enough food and rest are the best babies of all.

As your little ones grow, let them stick to the baby schedule as long as possible. The naps will end after kindergarten, but you can still put your kids to bed about 8 P.M. on school nights. The better they sleep, the better they'll do in school.

I've actually been to people's homes where kids are allowed to stay up all hours of the night. The children are often extremely active in the daytime, overcompensating, it appears, for their fatigue. Then the parents wonder why a teacher or some other authority figure would want to put their kids on a Ritalin regimen. Disciplining your kids is about disciplining yourself. Single mamas often have a tough time with this because we try to be so accommodating with our kids. Also, by the time we get home, tired and eager to have a few moments for ourselves, we often let the evening get away from us. By the time we look at the clock, it's already eight-thirty and we haven't even served dinner yet. Do not let this happen; it is the source of too many discipline problems.

Even if you set a good foundation, your kids, like all children, will behave inappropriately from time to time. I think it's important to identify what's important to each of your kids. For some, it's playing outside; for others, it's money or TV time. Whatever it is, that should be the thing you limit or take away from your child as punishment. No child wants to live without his favorite things.

I found that involving a child's father in the discipline process also helps. This is not an outlet available to all single mamas, but it's a wonderful resource if you have it. It's a good idea to share some of your children's inappropriate incidents with Daddy, but not necessarily all of them. You don't want to come across as someone who's totally helpless when it comes to dealing with behavior problems, but you do want your children to know that both their parents are concerned about their welfare.

If you're dating someone, you may want to consider his advice. It is never a good idea, however, to let him take over your discipline duties. Tell him you appreciate his concern, while making it clear that you are your children's disciplinarian. This does not mean your children shouldn't listen to reasonable requests from your boyfriend—or your girlfriends, for that matter. The kids should know that they are expected to respect all of your friends. But do not let every man who comes into your home play daddy; it just sets everyone in the household up for disappointment. If your man ever expresses interest in marrying you, and you take him seriously and you're interested, let him know that you'd expect him to ease into the stepfather role. Tell him that while the two of you work on your relationship, he can gradually find his place with your children. Meantime, however, it's your responsibility to make sure your kids are doing what they're supposed to do. As long as you remember basic things, like schedules and allowing your kids to share their feelings with you during appropriate times, this should not be a problem.

Often, men in the lives of single mamas do not understand parenting, let alone single parenting. They tend to think the women in their lives are far too lenient with the kids. This may come from a position of selfishness. If these men were used to dating single women with no kids, they expect to be the focus of their girlfriend's attention. With you, there's always some kid getting in the way. Many men let their jealousy and frustration guide their so-called attempts at discipline. Your boyfriend should be nothing more than an older friend to your kids; you and the child's father (if possible) are the parents. If your man does make a commitment to you and your children, then you can share with him how you think your children should be raised. It's okay to take ideas from him, but never okay to let him take over.

One of the best ways to make discipline work in your family is to be consistent. While you and your children's father may have totally different ways of providing discipline, I would suggest trying to

---

Getting Them to Behave

* Enroll in a parenting class (check with hospitals, community centers, and child welfare organizations).
* Get the kids involved in church activities.
* Give the kids time-outs.
* Take time-outs.
* Get them to bed early.
* Get them up early enough to have breakfast with them.
* Stick to rules and be consistent.
* Give them responsibilities.
* Read to them before bedtime.
* Talk to them at least ten minutes each day.
* Limit TV time to one hour after homework is done.

---

have some uniform methods for teaching the kids right from wrong. But even if your children's two families disagree, stick to your guns on your method. When your children tell you, "I don't have to do that at my dad's house," you tell them that's okay, but at your house, things will be done a certain way. When you see that trying to persuade your ex to accept your rearing methods is not going to happen, give it up. You should consider incorporating some of what works at his house in your own system. But whatever you do, don't go back and forth. The resulting inconsistency causes more confusion and insecurity in your children's lives.

Sharon

Sharon had two kids when she met J. T. He admired what a good mom Sharon seemed to be. She didn't yell at her kids, and yet they were very well behaved. Her oldest, Junior, only nine years old, played basketball with the finesse of a much older player. The kid had some serious moves.

Sharon had had other boyfriends, but they never understood how she raised her kids. Although she was white, the fathers of her two boys and her boyfriends were all African American. Sharon told me that the black men in her life believed that blacks and whites discipline their kids differently. Typically, they said, white parents are less strict, and black parents are better disciplinarians because they whip their kids.

When Sharon told me how much she appreciated that her new African-American boyfriend, J. T., didn't believe in beating children into submission, I urged her not to think of him as an exception. I told her that I've heard black people say whites are not as strict when it comes to discipline as blacks are, but I think a lot of that has to do with perspective. I think it is stereotypical to assume whites act one way and blacks another when it comes to getting kids to behave.

I think all single mamas should strive to take discipline beyond beatings. Beatings may have worked in the old days, but beatings also left scars. Beatings may have been appropriate for black children when their parents had to submit to unwritten rules about making a scene. Black children had few choices in the old days, and their parents couldn't afford to have them misbehaving in public. In school, they did better if they sat quietly, without challenging the teachers.

These days, our children must grow up disciplined, but not shackled. They must assert themselves and seek what is rightfully theirs. We send our children mixed messages if we beat them into submission and then expect them to be bright and inquisitive and to take chances.

I explained all this to Sharon, and I think she understood.

She told me that her other African-American boyfriends whipped her kids. I asked her why she allowed this, and she told me the boyfriends loved her and her kids. She said she thought of them as fathers.

Sharon had several boyfriends, and her children had to adapt to each of their styles. Often her boys lived in fear, not knowing how to behave, because what was okay with one boyfriend was taboo with the next.

I remember when I first met Junior. He was a friendly, outgoing

---

Discipline and Your Boyfriend

✴ Tell your children to obey any adult whose care you put them in, including your boyfriend's.

✴ You should be the primary disciplinarian; never say, "Go ask J. T." (or whomever).

✴ Do not let your boyfriend hit your children.

✴ If you and your boyfriend do not see eye to eye on discipline, know that he probably won't be a good stepfather.

---

boy, but sometimes he seemed to try too hard. Once I took him with Winston and a few other boys to a Chinese restaurant; before we got out of the car, Junior made some kind of racist remark about Chinese people. I immediately corrected him and explained how what he had said was racist and wrong. He was so sorry about what he'd said that he spent the entire evening making remarks about how nice and smart and clean the Chinese-American waiters were. It was obvious how easily this kid could lose himself trying to win the approval of a parent figure.

Whenever we'd go to Junior's house, he seemed to be a stranger in his own home. He spoke in hushed tones, always aware that if he said the wrong thing, he might offend his mother's boyfriend. Whenever J. T. said anything to Junior, the boy appeared to be walking on egg shells. It seemed he didn't want to anger his mother's boyfriend, because he knew how important the relationship was to his mother. This man may not have beat Junior, but he didn't have to because so many before him had already managed to undermine his self-confidence.

Mother of the Year

Ona has two boys, Jacob and Scooter. She was in her early twenties when she had them, and the boys' dad was in her life off and on.

Ona's biggest concern during her kids' early years was the health of her baby, Scooter.

Scooter was born with a deformed heart. He had to have surgery during the first weeks of his life, then several other operations after his first birthday. Had it not been for Scooter's incredible doctors, he could have died; instead, he was an energetic, bright child who lived to play. He loved all kinds of sports, and despite his heart condition, he played with vigor. A lot of that had to do with how Ona brought him up.

Ona has the potential to become the ideal "Single Mamahood" mother. She spent lots of time with her boys and made them the center of her world. Sometimes this would bother her boyfriend, but Ona stayed focused. She knew her boyfriend had not made a commitment to her; her priority was the kids. Ona was not working because Scooter's heart problem always got in the way of her jobs. He'd have to be in the hospital for weeks at a time, and the doctors always encouraged her to stay with him. They said his prognosis would be better with Mama at his side. Ona did not want her baby to die.

Each time Scooter was discharged from the hospital, he would return to his mother, and his brother, Jacob, and a life full of love. She would take the boys to the park and museums; she would read them bedtime stories and teach them their colors and numbers and letters. She always made them home-cooked meals and put them to bed on time.

Scooter had heart surgery again at age three. Doctors told Ona that if the procedure was successful, there would probably not be any more operations for several years. Ona and Jacob were there with Scooter every day during the week after the surgery. His recovery was successful.

A couple of weeks later, Ona enrolled in a special class offered by the state for mothers who were receiving welfare benefits and mothers of children enrolled in Head Start, a federal program for families living in poverty. Called "Survival Skills for Women," it was a ten-week course that taught women about how to find a job, how to write a resumé and how to conduct themselves during a job

Poverty and Parenting

Being poor may make parenting difficult, but it does not mean you cannot become a super single mama. The most important thing to do is to strive to be the best you can be.

There are many resources available to poor single mamas. There's church and lots of social service programs. Head Start is one of the best.

I was in the first class of Head Start kids. It helped me so much. It exposed me to education and structure at a very early age. I knew how to read when I entered kindergarten.

These days, Head Start has programs for single mamas, as well as for their children. The parenting classes and job preparation classes are priceless.

If you are poor and you feel you have no other resources, find the Head Start program or an equivalent social service program in your neighborhood—and get involved.

interview. It taught them how to dress at work and how to interact with their coworkers and bosses. Another segment of the course was designed to teach parenting skills.

The parenting portion of the class allowed the women to offer each other advice on what worked and what did not work for them. I was invited to speak to the class, and I was surprised to find Leon's mother was enrolled also. Both these women were great mothers; they put their personal career goals on the back burner until they'd done all they could for their kids. Other women in the class had become pregnant as teens or while in their early twenties, and they were, for the most part, unskilled. But changes in the welfare system forced them to discover that they actually did have abilities that could land them work. Ona was an active participant in the parenting part of the class. She'd often find herself offering advice about how to keep kids on track, how to make them feel secure, and how to discipline them without beating them. Until her exposure to the women in the class, she had no idea how few single women dealt with their kids the way she did.

When the class ended, Ona and some of the other students were invited to a banquet sponsored by Head Start. The purpose of the dinner was to celebrate the accomplishments of some of the teachers and staff members who'd just completed the semester. Ona had no idea one of the awards was a plaque with her name inscribed on it. Above her name was the inscription MOTHER OF THE YEAR.

18

Giving Up Custody

Some day, my son may decide he wants to live with his father. This is a reality I think about every time one of my single-mama friends has to deal with the issue. I've also spoken to a lot of the fathers of these children. Fortunately, the fathers I know are the kinds of dads who take responsibility for their kids; they keep their children during summers and frequently during the year on weekends and during school vacations. These are dads who'd be delighted at the possibility of being able to have more permanent custody.

My only advice to you is that if your children want to live with their father, listen to them, and give it serious consideration. Of course, some kids will say they want to live with their father to be manipulative, as a means of getting their way. But there will be times when they are dead serious.

Be Realistic and Honest

When Winston asked me how I'd feel about his going to live with his dad, I told him I'd miss him terribly, but that if he felt it was best for him to be with his father at a certain point in his life, he probably should be there. I also explained that he'd have to consider the demands he would be putting on his custodial parent.

I told Winston that his dad's schedule makes it very difficult for him to be there every day at the same time after school to make sure he gets to his practices and games on time. I told him to keep in mind that if he went to live with his father, both he and his dad would have to make sacrifices.

The Break May Be Good

I know of many cases of a mother sending her preteen or teenage boy to live with his father. Usually the single mama is facing some male issues that are beyond the scope of her gender. These are cases where the boy is hanging around with the wrong crowd; he's flirting with the idea of joining a gang or he's experimenting with drugs or he's combative or violent. These are cases where a boy might be better off with his dad. I also know of situations where girls have been hard to deal with or are experiencing changes a single mama feels uncomfortable with handling on her own. Again, the child is usually going through puberty or is well into her teen years. These are cases where the girl may be hanging around with the wrong crowd, spending time with gang bangers, experimenting with drugs and/or sex or dating an older boy or a young man. Sometimes girls and boys who are at a rough crossroads in the growing process think living with Dad will be easier. Often, time with Dad does do them some good, but mostly, it just gives them the breather they need to get their heads together. But, despite where they live, if kids do not get the discipline they need from either Dad or Mom, they will be insecure and often they'll have low self-esteem and make bad decisions.

When your kids start talking about going to live with Dad, the first thing you need to do is listen. Do the kind of active listening I talked about in the "Help!" chapter. Find out how the kid is feeling and why. Let the child know that you'd like to share his or her concerns with your ex. If possible, you should all get together and talk; that way, you won't be the bad guy and your child will have a difficult time playing his or her parents against one another. The child will feel loved at a very vulnerable time, and that's extremely important.

When They Want to Live With Daddy

✸ Take them seriously.

✸ Hear them out.

✸ Call a family meeting.

✸ Don't get emotional, but be honest about your feelings.

✸ Make a plan.

✸ Get your ego out of it.

✸ Give it a chance.

✸ Be ready for them to come back. They often do.

Be open about any concerns you may have about the child going to live with his or her father. Do not get all self-righteous and act like you wear a parenting halo. This is a time to listen and to love unconditionally and to do what's really best for your child.

Sometimes It's Mama's Idea

There will be other times when the issues of your child going to live with Daddy might come up. There may be a time in your life when you're the one who makes the request. What if you need time to finish college or law school or a residency program? What if you're in the military and you have to serve some time overseas? Or what if you get a special assignment at work that will require a lot of time and travel? These are times when the child may very well need to be with Daddy. Often single mamas decide that their child should live with Grandma during times like this; they don't even involve the father in the decision. This is wrong. If you can't be the custodial parent, the father should be the first person you consider. If you suspect he's not up to the responsibility, talk to him in an open, honest, nonconfrontational way about your concerns. Be detailed about what the custodial parent's job entails. Spell out the demands of a typical week. If he thinks he can handle it, there's really no reason he shouldn't have a chance to try. But let him know that you won't be angry at him if it doesn't work out. Work out a Plan B with him, just in case.

As a single mama, you cannot be selfish. You cannot expect everything to go your way. Put your children and their needs first at all times. In the end, you will all win, but your kids will benefit the most.

Chuck and Dria

Chuck's baby's mama Dria was about ten years his junior. She'd hoped the baby would bring the two of them closer together, but the opposite happened. Chuck paid child support and wanted his daughter to be with him as much as possible, but Dria wasn't having any of it.

Although the two of them lived in the same town, Dria would take her daughter to her mother's house when she was going to be out of town. She was dating a professional football player at the time, and she tried to make all of his "away" games, which meant she was out of town a lot during football season.

Chuck had the hardest time trying to see the baby. The grandmother, fearful of angering her daughter, never allowed Chuck to take his baby away from her home.

Dria would ignore Chuck's phone calls and lash out at him whenever he tried to discuss the issue with her.

Chuck and I were good friends, and I could see how much all of this was getting to him. I often thought about the baby and all that she was missing by not being able to spend time with her daddy and his family. Chuck's mother and sister were heartbroken over the situation. I suggested to Chuck that he see an attorney about getting forced visitation.

Chuck's attorney not only established the visitation but pointed out to Chuck that he was paying well above the state's minimum standards of child support. When Chuck said he didn't mind paying the extra money, his attorney explained that if the judge ruled in his favor, he'd have his child a lot more and would need the extra money in order to care for her. In the end, Chuck's ex was ordered to have her child ready to be picked up by her dad every other

Daddies Have Rights, Too

If your children's father wants more time with your children do not look at it as a threat but a blessing.

Unless your ex wants full custody, and you think it's in the best interest of the kids to have you as their custodial parent, think about a way to share custody. If your ex is the type of man who can successfully care for children full time, he's probably reasonable enough to sit down with you to work something out. If necessary, bring in a third party, an objective person who can help you mediate a solution.

weekend, every other major holiday, and during the summer, when the baby would be with her father for six weeks. Not only that, the child support was reduced.

In the beginning, Dria was one angry young woman. But after about six months, she got over it, and she got used to it. She even began making it a habit to call Chuck when something came up during the week and she needed someone to keep the baby for a few hours. After a couple of years, Chuck and his ex are on good terms, and their daughter is better off because of it.

19

Special Times

For most single mamas, assuming head-of-household responsibilities requires unselfish love, lots of time for her child, and,
quite frankly, very little time for her own pursuits. This does not
mean a single mama is a martyr. It does mean, for the most part, that
she is not like one of her single friends. She can't go out to clubs for
happy hour every Friday night. If her children are having a Saturday-
night sleepover, she'll have to say no thanks to friends who invite
her out for a party. Being a single mama is a paradox. You're far
more mama than single, however, for the sake of your children and
the generations ahead of them.

What do your children like to do with their spare time? Each of
them is different. Does one like to read, the other enjoy renting
movies, and another like to go out to dinner? You should know, and
you should make it a point to spend time with each of your kids at
least once a month doing that special something. If it's impossible
to give each child individual time, do things together, but make each
day special for one at a time. In other words, May can be Terry's
month, where everyone goes to the park on Saturday during the
month to play and then out for ice cream. October can be for Sandy,
where the whole family catches a movie on the weekends.

Special times are good for building self-esteem. They remind your kids that they are special and that despite the fact that their mother is a single mama, she knows how to recognize what's special about each of her kids. Special times build family cohesiveness, a sense of ritual and tradition.

Nuclear families, where Mom and Dad live under the same roof, already have established rituals that work for them. Few, if any, of those rituals, may work well for the single-mama-headed household, so you have to create your own.

Plan special field trips or backyard camping trips or parties for your kids when they lose a tooth. Have parties for their favorite dolls or toys. Invite their friends. They might express embarrassment, but inside they'll be beaming with pride. Make your family official.

Attend church services regularly with the kids. Hold Bible studies at your home. Have the kids participate in youth group activities at church. Let them become a part of a church family. If at all possible, do your shopping for a spiritual home while your kids are still young. Frequently changing churches will do nothing for building the kind of stability your kids need. Also, as a family, do things to help others. Visit shut-ins and others in need. Let your children see you giving to others. You'll be planting seeds for a strong, long-lasting bond between you and the children. (See Peace, Love, and Spirituality chapter.)

Take family trips. You don't have to spend a lot of money or go to exotic places. Label a special jar for saving small change. It can be cashed in at the bank from time to time and added to a special vacation fund.

When you tell your children you're going to take them someplace or to do something for them, keep your promise. Kids rarely remember promises kept, but they always remember those we break. Make it a habit to keep your dreams of what you'd like to do for them to yourself. Only voice those things you're sure you can accomplish.

Special times can be attending those goofy school plays kids have or making it to open house at school or to a parent-teacher conference. These things mean so much to your children, but often, a busy single mama forgets. As soon as you read a note from school about one of these meetings, put the date in your calendar. You must do everything in your power to be there. If you have to, trade an off day at work with a friend. Most of the meetings are set at times that are convenient for most parents. So whatever you do, do not go on a date or out with a girlfriend when you should be at your kids' school for something. Your children will never forgive you.

If your kids play sports, you should make every effort to be there, too. During baseball season, I am a slave to my son. He looks up in the stands to make sure I'm there before he goes up to bat. If he hears my big mouth yelling for him to hit a home run, I almost see a smile forming at his mouth. Sure, he's embarrassed, but at the same time, he's proud. Someone who loves him is there for him to give him the support he needs. If you can't make it, explain why.

Also, do what you can to make sure your children's father is there for some of those special occasions. Even if he lives out of town, see if the two of you can work something out so that you both show up for the first parent-teacher meeting or for some of your children's special recitals and games. This may sound as though I'm asking you to do the impossible. I know how a single mama can feel about her children's father. But if you've been following the reasoning in this book, by now you should understand that these kinds of things can work out. Remember, you're sacrificing; you're giving up something for the sake of your children, even if the only thing you're sacrificing is your pride.

It's also important to allow your children's stepfamily to share in special occasions. How much you may dislike the new wife or her old mother is beside the point. You should be able to grin and bear it through an hour or two, or even through dinner, for the sake of your kids. There's no need for you to get all bent out of shape over people your children have chosen to love. Keep your feelings to yourself. Remember, your feelings of jealousy or insecurity are weaknesses. To break the cycle of single mamahood, your kids have to learn to be bigger emotionally than their mother, and it's your job to help them be bigger.

Ironically, I've found these times are normally much tougher on the stepmother than they are on the single mama. It's her "perfect" family that's threatened when her husband's children by another woman are on the scene. She'll have to do far more adjusting than you will. But here, too, do what you can to keep the peace. This is not for you; it's for the kids.

Some of the most important moments in your children's lives can be ruined all because the parents and stepparents aren't mature enough, even for a few hours, to forget their animosity toward one another. Yet, some of the most beautiful graduations and weddings have been those where the children are fortunate enough to have the presence of every family member that loves them.

Mother's Day

Mother's Day is always a special day at our house. The funny thing is, I never expected it to be. When I was a kid, we never made a big deal out of Mother's Day. Sure, we'd give our mother the card we made at school, if we remembered to bring it home. Later, after she and Leon married, he'd buy her a gift. But my mother's birthday is so close to Mother's Day, we always celebrate the two together.

Winston only knows when my birthday rolls around because I remind him. But he never forgets Mother's Day. He always does it up in a big way.

The first big fuss he made was when he was eight. I was fast asleep when Winston knocked in my door with a surprise. It was breakfast in bed—a Pop Tart, Slimfast bar, a toaster waffle, bowl of cereal, banana, and orange juice. Of course, I cried. He also surprised me with a poem he' written earlier in the week.

Every year since then, he's given me something special that he made or bought with his allowance. Later in the morning, we go to church together, where he gets a flower from his Sunday school teacher or makes me something special. Mother's Day, the way Winston does it, is our own family ritual.

A Special Game

I never thought that the baseball season of 1997, when I was feeling sad for Winston, would end so special. I'd spoken to Teddy several times about how great it would be if he could come to Florida to attend one of Winston's games. There was only one more game of the season, and I didn't expect to hear from him, but he called.

"Kelly, I can come down there this weekend," he said. It was too good to be true. I didn't want to tell Winston, just in case, but I couldn't resist. He was so excited, he told all his friends. Charlie, Drew, and Jacob couldn't wait to see Winston's dad. Since I'd attended all of Winston's games alone, a lot of the parents also wanted to see him, mostly just out of curiosity.

The plan was for Teddy to pick up Winston from school that Friday and spend the afternoon with him. I even told Teddy he could stay at our house (in the guest room) for the weekend so that he and Winston could spend more time together. He'd take him to the game the next day, then perhaps to his school for an end-of-spring field day, and if there was time, he'd go to church with us on Sunday.

That Friday, I told Winston what to do if, by any chance, Teddy didn't show up on time. He'd call me and then go over to the recreation center and wait for me to get off so that I could pick him up. Somehow, that morning, when I got a telephone message saying Teddy had missed his flight, I was not surprised. The message was not clear. I wasn't sure if he'd be in Tampa by four thirty or if his flight was departing at that time. I tried paging him, but by the time he called me back, I was out on assignment. I called Winston's school to leave a message for him to take the bus home. I knew he'd be disappointed and confused.

That afternoon, around four thirty, Winston called me to tell me he was home. I explained that Teddy was still coming, but that I wasn't sure what time. Winston asked me for permission to go down the street to play street hockey with his friends. I'd only allowed him to do that one other time when I wasn't home, but since I knew he was trying to work off the anxiety, I said it was okay.

Five minutes later, I got a call from Teddy. He'd arrived and was in a rental car headed toward St. Petersburg.

I guided him to our house, because he wasn't sure how to get there. When he got to the housing community's security gate, he handed the phone to the security guard so I could tell him it was okay to let Teddy in. Then I directed him to the street where Winston plays hockey with his friends.

"I see him," Teddy said.

"Wait," I told him. "I want to see what happens."

"Daddy!" I heard Winston yell. I saw them embrace, and I knew it was safe to say goodbye.

I spent most of that night at a friend's house. The next morning, I was awakened by cartoons and Winston and Teddy's laughter. I put on my robe and gave Teddy a hug. I almost cried. The three of us had breakfast together at a restaurant; then I went about my business.

By the time I arrived home early the next morning, Teddy's alarm was going off. It was time for him to get ready for his flight. I thanked him and asked him to visit Winston more often.

When he left, I went into Winston's room; he was fast asleep. I knew Teddy's visit had meant the world to him. I wondered whether he'd made a base hit, whether he'd struck out or made his first home run. Either way, I knew he was okay, because for the first time, his daddy was there with him at his baseball game, and that's all that really mattered.

APPENDIX

Dos and Don'ts of Single Mamahood

* Have a positive attitude about being a single mama.
* Be honest with your children.
* Do not say anything negative about the daddy.
* Do not have emotional breakdowns in front of your children.
* Take care of your emotional needs.
* Take care of your children's emotional needs.
* Love yourself.
* Remind your children often that you love them.
* Learn from others.
* Don't be afraid to get professional help.
* Don't get in the habit of letting your children sleep in your bed.
* Listen to your children, and respect their feelings.
* Don't blame all your children's problems on the fact that you're a single mama.
* Don't let your ex in and out of your life.
* Don't be desperate to find a new man.

* Take your time in new relationships.

* Don't let your children see a man come out of your bedroom in the morning.

* Consider your children's feelings about your significant other.

* Expect to make choices between your job and children.

* Choose your job when necessary.

* Don't tell your boss and coworkers all your personal business.

* Don't feel guilty about your work.

* Have a list of baby sitters "on call."

* Get involved in your child's school life.

* Put your children to bed early, and wake them early enough to have breakfast with them.

* Read to little children at night.

* Involve your children in sports and club activities.

* Support the children by attending their special events.

* Budget your money and spend wisely.

* Do what you can to collect child support.

* Encourage regular Daddy visitation.

* Be firm with your children and consistent with discipline.

* Join a church and attend services regularly.

* Be civil and understanding with your ex, his family and significant other.

* Don't allow your friends and family to bad mouth your ex and his family.

* Establish family rituals.

Index